♦ SAIS Papers in Latin American Studies ♦
Sponsored by the Central American and Caribbean Program

Development Postponed

The Political Economy of Central America in the 1980s

◆ **SAIS Papers in Latin American Studies** ◆

Sponsored by the Central American and Caribbean Program

◆ *Bruce M. Bagley, Series Editor* ◆

Development Postponed: The Political Economy of Central America in the 1980s, Richard E. Feinberg and Bruce M. Bagley

State and Society in Contemporary Colombia: Beyond the National Front, edited by Bruce M. Bagley, Francisco E. Thoumi, and Juan G. Tokatlian

♦ About the Book and Authors ♦

The collapse of political institutions and the failure of economic development models in Central America have turned the region into an ideological battleground. Central Americans are now debating—and fighting over—different conceptions of how to constitute society, the best way to organize production and to distribute benefits, and the political structures best suited to protecting the region's security and ensuring its future prosperity. This book examines the economic and political roots of the current crisis, reviewing the different strategies governments have adopted to cope with their financial woes and evaluating the role that international financial assistance has played in postponing adjustment to the crisis. The region's economies are carefully analyzed to highlight sectors with the potential to generate recovery and growth, and the larger political economy models that might direct the development process are also evaluated. The authors close with a discussion of the fundamental question: Can a Central America composed of a heterogeneous mix of national political economies live at peace with itself and the world?

Richard E. Feinberg is vice president of the Overseas Development Council. **Bruce M. Bagley** is associate professor of comparative politics and acting director of the Latin American Studies Program of the School of Advanced International Studies, The Johns Hopkins University. He is coeditor of *Contadora and the Central American Peace Process* (Westview, 1985).

*This volume in the
SAIS Papers in Latin American Studies
is published in cooperation with the
Overseas Development Council*

About the Overseas Development Council

The Overseas Development Council is an independent, nonprofit organization established in 1969 to increase American understanding of the economic and social problems confronting the developing countries and to promote awareness of the importance of these countries to the United States in an increasingly interdependent international system.

In pursuit of these goals, ODC functions as a center for policy analysis, a forum for the exchange of ideas, and a resource for public education. Current projects fall within four broad areas of policy concern: trade and industrial policy, international financial issues, development strategies and development cooperation, and political and strategic aspects of U.S. economic relations with the Third World.

ODC's program is funded by foundations, corporations, and private individuals; its policies are determined by a governing Board and Council. In the selection and coverage of issues addressed by the current ODC program, including the U.S.-Third World Policy Perspectives series, the ODC staff and Board also benefit from the advice of members of the ODC Program Advisory Committee.

Development Postponed

The Political Economy of Central America in the 1980s

Richard E. Feinberg and Bruce M. Bagley

Routledge
Taylor & Francis Group

LONDON AND NEW YORK

First published 1986 by Westview Press, Inc.

Published 2018 by Routledge
52 Vanderbilt Avenue, New York, NY 10017
2 Park Square, Milton Park, Abingdon, Oxon OX14 4RN

Routledge is an imprint of the Taylor & Francis Group, an informa business

Copyright © 1986 Taylor & Francis

All rights reserved. No part of this book may be reprinted or reproduced or utilised in any form or by any electronic, mechanical, or other means, now known or hereafter invented, including photocopying and recording, or in any information storage or retrieval system, without permission in writing from the publishers.

Notice:
Product or corporate names may be trademarks or registered trademarks, and are used only for identification and explanation without intent to infringe.

Library of Congress Cataloging in Publication Data
Feinberg, Richard E.
  Development postponed.
  (SAIS Papers in Latin American Studies)
  Bibliography: p.
  1. Central America—Economic conditions. 2. Central America—Politics and government. 3. Economic stabilization—Central America. I. Bagley, Bruce Michael. II Title. III. Series.
  HC141.F45 1986   338.9728   86-4038
ISBN 13: 978-0-367-01062-1 (hbk)
ISBN 13: 978-0-367-16049-4 (pbk)

Contents

List of Tables ix
Preface xi

1. Background to the Crisis 1
   Introduction 1
   Seeds of Conflict 2
      Political Destabilization 2
      Uneven Economic Development 3
      Structural Flaws 3
      The Global Recession 4

2. Financial Stabilization and Structural
   Change, *Richard E. Feinberg* 5
   The Medium-Term Outlook: Prolonged Austerity 5
      Trade 5
      Debt 7
      External Capital Flows 7
         Private Credit 9
         Bilateral Donors 9
         Multilateral Sources 11
      Domestic Savings and Investment 12
   The Postponement of Economic Stabilization 13
      The Role of Government 13
      Gradualism Versus "Shock Treatment" 16
   Structural Adjustment in the Future 20
      Traditional Agricultural Exports 21
      Agroindustry 22

vii

　　　　Transformation Industries (Export-
　　　　　　oriented Light Manufactures) 24
　　　　Industrial Production: A Revived Central
　　　　　　American Common Market 24
　　　　　　Tariff Reform 26
　　　　　　Improved Liquidity 27
　　　　　　Balance of Trade 27
　　　　　　Recapitalizing CABEI 27
　　　　The Production of Basic Grains and
　　　　　　Essentials for the Domestic Market 28

3. **Economic Growth and Political Order,**
　　Bruce M. Bagley 31

　　　　Alternative Political Economies 32
　　　　　　Democracy-with-Liberty 33
　　　　　　Democracy-with-Justice 35
　　　　　　Revolutionary Democracy 39
　　　　Conflict or Coexistence? 41
　　　　　　The Contadora Affirmative 42
　　　　　　The Alternative of Low-Intensity Warfare 43
　　　　External Aid, Capital Swamping, and
　　　　　　Structural Dependency 44

4. **Summary and Conclusions** 47

Notes 51
List of Conference Participants 61
Other Books Published by the Overseas
　　Development Council 64
Other Books Published by the
　　Latin American Studies Program 65

Tables

1. Per capita growth rates, 1980-1985 6

2. GNP predictions, 1986-1988 6

3. Debt service: Interest payments as a percentage of exports of goods and services, 1979-1984 8

4. U.S. foreign assistance to Central America, FY 1983-1986 10

5. Gross domestic investment by dollars 12

6. The size of government: Central government expenditure as percentage of GDP, 1979-1984 14

7. Central government overall deficit as a percentage of GDP, 1979-1984 15

8. Central American Common Market exports, 1980-1984 25

Preface

Most of the debate on the Central American crisis has centered around politics (human rights violations, elections) and international diplomacy (the competition among external powers for influence in the region). Yet, both the roots of the crisis and its long-term solutions lie to an important degree in economics—or better stated, in political economy. The highly uneven patterns of economic development in past decades generated the emerging middle classes and popular movements that are pressing for a new political order. Economic choices will also determine to a great degree the future shape of Central American societies and their relations to the wider world.

To focus greater attention on the economics of the region, the Overseas Development Council (ODC) and the Central American and Caribbean Program of The Johns Hopkins University School of Advanced International Studies (SAIS) organized a series of meetings in Washington, D.C., on May 14–16, 1984, to bring together experts from Central America and the United States to exchange views on "Alternative Economic Strategies for Central America and the Implications for U.S. Policy." The main conference was open to the public, and some 250 people attended. The expert participants also had the opportunity to exchange opinions in private seminars with officials and staff members from the World Bank, the Inter-American Development Bank, and the U.S. Agency for International Development (USAID).[1]

The conference exposed the Washington policy community to the broad range of opinions currently being aired in Central America. This book does not seek to impose an artificial consensus that denies this diversity. Rather, it reflects our own interpretation, as chairmen, of the main themes of the conference, subsequently enriched by a personal visit to the region in early 1985. In the belief that much more work is required to raise the level of knowledge and understanding of the Central American economies, this book also attempts to pinpoint areas of disagreement or ignorance where future research is badly needed.

We are not among those who believe that vital security interests of the United States are necessarily at stake in Central America. The region is militarily weak and economically poor. Strategically, precisely because of its proximity to the United States and distance from Eurasia, the region is less exposed to Soviet military threats than are other areas of the Third World. Nor is Central America of great consequence in the global struggle of ideas, although it has become an arena of East-West tensions.

Rather, we focus attention on the region because it is at a historic juncture where the destiny of some 22 million individuals—and possibly that of their successor generations—is being decided. As social scientists, we hope that our work can contribute, however marginally, to elucidating the options the region faces and thereby can promote better choices by the region's leaders and elicit better advice from influential foreign governments.

Funding for the conference was generously provided by Marjorie Benton; the Benton Foundation; the Inter-American Foundation; NCR Corporation; InterNorth, Inc.; and Caribbean/Central American Action. The Ford Foundation provided a follow-on grant that enabled us to visit Central America to discuss a preliminary draft with scholars, business leaders, politicians, and government officials and to publish and disseminate this book. We are greatly indebted to many North Americans and Central Americans for their commentaries. Special appreciation is due to Christine Bindert, Xabier Gorostiaga, Luis Landau, William Leo Grande, Richard Newfarmer, Robert Pastor, Lucy Schwank, Cathryn Thorup, and Juan Tokatlian for their insightful criticisms of an earlier draft of this book. The responsibility for the views presented here, however, is solely our own.

Richard E. Feinberg
Overseas Development Council

Bruce M. Bagley
The Johns Hopkins University School of
Advanced International Studies

Washington, D.C.
September 15, 1985

◆ *SAIS Papers in Latin American Studies* ◆
Sponsored by the Central American and Caribbean Program

Development Postponed

The Political Economy of Central America in the 1980s

1
Background to the Crisis

INTRODUCTION

Central America is passing through an extremely painful but potentially creative period. The collapse of political institutions and economic development models has turned the region into an ideological battleground. Central Americans are now debating—and fighting over—different conceptions of how to constitute society, the proper relationship between the individual and the state, how best to organize production and to distribute its fruits, and the diplomacy that would best protect the region's security and contribute to its future prosperity. Poor choices—or a chronic failure to build consensus—will produce more years of human suffering and continued economic decline. Wise choices could lay the foundation for a new era of political stability and economic growth.

Later in this chapter we will briefly examine the economic and political roots of the current crisis. Chapter 2 first considers the different strategies that governments have adopted to cope with the resulting financial squeezes and the role that foreign aid has played in permitting the postponement of adjustment measures. It then dissects the region's economies to highlight the economic sectors that could become the engines of recovery and growth in a brighter future. External, domestic, and regional markets are compared for their buoyancy and openness to various Central American products. Drawing heavily on the papers and discussions of the conference "Alternative Economic Development Strategies for Central America and the Implications for U.S. Policy," Chapter 2 also estimates the medium-term outlook for trade and capital flows in order to set parameters on the likely pace of economic development.

The discussion is broadened in Chapter 3 to consider the larger political economy models that might direct this development process. Political models—with different mixes of control and participation—are linked to corresponding economic models with public and private sectors of varying strength. External pressures and domestic legitimacy requirements constrain Central Americans to choices that are narrower than theory allows, but that still present substantial distinctions. In recognition of the fact that the region today is more politically diverse than in the past, the final section of Chapter 3 focuses on the fundamental question: Can a Central America divided into a heterogeneous mix of national political economies live at peace with itself and the world?

Chapter 4 is a summation of the various problems confronting Central America. It concludes with a discussion of the individual courses that the countries will need to undertake to restore growth and ensure peace.

SEEDS OF CONFLICT

Central America's crisis is not the result of economic stagnation. On the contrary, the crisis has its origins in the impressive—and uneven—growth that the region witnessed between 1950 and 1978. The clash between growing economies and stagnant political institutions produced systemic fissures. These fissures were widened by the uneven distribution of the new wealth. The current recession and debt crisis have simply exacerbated existing tensions.

POLITICAL DESTABILIZATION

Almost three decades of economic expansion generated new social forces not content with the political *status quo* in most of the countries of the region (Costa Rica and, to a degree, Honduras being the exceptions). Moreover, a demographic boom produced a population younger, better educated, and more aware of their countries' political shortcomings and of the world's possibilities. In the rural areas, the expansion of commercial, export-oriented agriculture displaced thousands of traditionally passive *campesinos* of the old *latifundia* system and sent them flooding into the cities to swell the ranks of the urban poor while creating a new group of more politically conscious salaried farm laborers who began to organize. Simultaneously, the birth of new industries led to the development of an urban labor movement.

The political leadership for these new groups emerged from the universities, the church, and the expanding urban middle class. With the notable exception of democratic Costa Rica, these emergent forces were generally denied effective participation in power, generating resentments and frustrations that led to the formation of militant opposition movements and armed guerrilla organizations. In reaction to the traditional, *status quo* orientation of U.S. policy in the region, such movements have often adopted an anti-imperialist rhetoric.[2]

UNEVEN ECONOMIC DEVELOPMENT

The fruits of economic expansion were unequally shared. Some progress was made in addressing the symptoms of poverty: For example, the adult literacy rate regionwide rose from 44 percent in 1960 to 72 percent in 1976. Nevertheless, the United Nations Economic Commission for Latin America (ECLA) estimated recently that 42 percent of the population of Central America (including Panama) lives in a state of "extreme poverty."[3] Extreme inequalities greatly exacerbated social and political tensions in Nicaragua, El Salvador, and Guatemala.

STRUCTURAL FLAWS

Industry grew rapidly after the founding of the Central American Common Market (CACM) in 1960. However, germinating in the "hothouse" security provided by high protective tariffs, Central American industry produced high-priced goods that could not be sold on international markets but that nevertheless required a high proportion of imported inputs. Local industry, therefore, failed to have the anticipated beneficial effect on the balance of payments. Being relatively capital intensive, industry also failed to absorb as much labor as some had hoped. In addition, the scarce financial resources that did exist went to industry and export agriculture rather than to the smaller-scale farmers who produced basic grains for local consumption. Whereas Central America as a whole was virtually self-sufficient in agriculture in the late 1960s, by the late 1970s the region was diverting increasing amounts of scarce foreign exchange for food imports.[4]

THE GLOBAL RECESSION

Being highly open economies tightly integrated into global markets, the countries of Central America were hit hard by the "shocks" of the 1970s and 1980s—high oil prices, skyrocketing interest rates, and the recession of 1980 to 1982. As a result of weak international prices for the region's main exports—coffee, cotton, bananas, sugar, and beef—by 1982 one unit of the region's exports was able to purchase only 74 percent of the imports it had purchased in 1979. Moreover, high interest rates increased the burden of a burgeoning foreign debt that began to eat up a sizable percentage of foreign exchange receipts.[5]

These four causes of the crisis—political unrest, uneven development, structural flaws in development strategies, and the global recession—have been self-reinforcing. Political unrest has undermined investor confidence and produced massive capital flight that, in turn, reduces employment and income levels and potentially further inflames political passions.

2
Financial Stabilization and Structural Change
Richard E. Feinberg

THE MEDIUM-TERM OUTLOOK: PROLONGED AUSTERITY

Central Americans have already suffered through half a decade of sharply declining living standards. From 1978 to 1984, per capita production fell by about 30 percent, and by another 3 percent in 1985 (see Table 1). Although most Central American economies seem to have reached a trough in 1983-1984, the per capita income of many Central Americans continues to fall as a result of rapid population growth, inflation, and high unemployment.

A definitive turning point for the region's fortunes is not yet in sight. On the contrary, the prospects for crucial trade and capital flows are discomforting, and growth prospects are further constrained by the foreign debt overhang and the drop in domestic investment. As a result, the Inter-American Development Bank, for example, has predicted average GNP growth rates of about 2 percent for 1986-1988 (see Table 2); given that the Central American populations grow at around 3.5 percent annually, living standards may continue to slip.

TRADE

The Central American economies are substantially driven by their external performance. Much of the pessimism regarding the region's medium-term outlook derives from the chronically unfavorable conditions on international markets for key Central

TABLE 1. PER CAPITA GROWTH RATES, 1980-1985
(percentage)

	1981	1982	1983	1984	1985^e	Accumulated Decline, 1980-1985^e
Guatemala	-1.8	-6.1	-5.5	-2.4	-4.2	-18.5
El Salvador	-11.0	-8.4	-3.8	-1.5	-1.4	-23.8
Honduras	-2.8	-4.0	-4.5	-0.8	-1.7	-13.0
Nicaragua	2.0	-4.4	1.3	-4.8	-5.9	-11.6
Costa Rica	-5.0	-9.7	-0.4	3.4	-2.5	-13.8
Central America^a	-3.7	-6.5	-2.6	-1.2	-3.1	-16.1

^{e} = estimate
^{a} = simple average

Source: United Nations Economic Commission for Latin America, Balance Preliminar de la Economica Latinoamericano, 1985, Santiago: ECLA, December 1985.

TABLE 2. GNP PREDICTIONS, 1986-1988

(Percentage)

	1986	1987	1988
Guatemala	2.7	3.1	3.5
El Salvador	2.0	2.5	3.0
Honduras	0.5	2.4	1.4
Nicaragua	0.8	1.4	0.3
Costa Rica	2.7	2.8	2.3
Central America (a)	1.7	2.4	2.1

(a) = simple average

Source: Inter-American Development Bank (IDB), "Financial Outlook of the Central American Bank for Economic Integration," Washington, D.C., 1984, p. 15.

American products. The region's terms of trade deteriorated by about 40 percent between 1977 and 1983; despite some probable secular improvement in the prices for coffee and meat, the region's overall terms of trade may not recover in the next several years.* Although nontraditional exports may enjoy more advantageous market prospects, their weight in overall exports is slight. Thus, even if the Caribbean Basin Initiative (CBI) helps stimulate a rapid increase in nontraditional exports to the United States, it will be several years before the effect can substantially improve countries' balance of payments.[6]

DEBT

To these problems in the trade account must be added a new burden: As a result of sharply increased levels of borrowing since the late 1970s, debt service requirements have risen dramatically. Scheduled interest payments alone account for about 15-20 percent of the export earnings of El Salvador and Honduras and for much higher percentages for the two countries that borrowed most heavily on private capital markets, Costa Rica and Nicaragua (see Table 3).

EXTERNAL CAPITAL FLOWS

The region's combined economic and political crises stimulated sharp increases in external capital flows that have helped nations to maintain import levels while meeting debt service. These capital inflows, however, have not fully compensated for the deterioration in the terms of trade, the inflated debt service burden, and the massive outflow of private capital. Moreover, although several important uncertainties make predictions hazardous, it seems unlikely that net external capital inflows will grow dramatically over the next several years. Private creditors are discouraged by political uncertainties and foreign exchange

---

*Subsequent to the writing of this book, world coffee prices have jumped substantially in response to a frost that injured Brazil's coffee crop. This will produce a considerable but temporary increase in foreign exchange earnings for Central America. In 1986 the region's terms of trade will also be assisted by the precipitous decline in oil prices and, perhaps, by the declining dollar.

TABLE 3. DEBT SERVICE: INTEREST PAYMENTS AS A PERCENTAGE OF EXPORTS OF GOODS AND SERVICES, 1979-1984

	1979	1980	1981	1982	1983	1984	1985* (e)
El Salvador	5.3	6.5	7.5	11.9	14.2	15.0	14.0
Guatemala	3.1	5.3	7.5	7.8	10.1	9.9	11.5
Costa Rica	12.8	18.0	25.5	33.4	41.8	37.4	28.0
Nicaragua (1)	5.5	7.4	15.6	31.0	34.0	43.0	N.A.
Honduras	8.6	10.6	14.5	22.4	17.7	19.0	17.0

* All revised figures from CEPAL, Preliminary Balance 1985.

(e) = preliminary estimate

(1) Total accrued interest payment to exports of goods and nonfactor services.

Sources: World Bank; International Monetary Fund; Inter-American Development Bank; Comisión Económica para América Latina, Preliminary Overview of the Latin American Economy. Santiago: CEPAL, 1984, 1985; central banks of El Salvador, Guatemala, and Honduras; Nicaraguan Ministry of Planning; and Consejeros Económicos y Financieros for data on Costa Rica.

shortages. Bilateral donors are already very active. Multilateral financial institutions are awaiting the establishment of stronger governments able to impose difficult economic reforms.

Estimates of the future external financing needs for Central America vary depending upon assumptions regarding regional export revenues, domestic savings and investment rates, and the efficiency of investment. However, even optimistic assumptions yield a high demand for external finance. Luis Rene Caceres of the Central American Bank for Economic Integration (CABEI) has estimated that if exports grow at 4 percent in real terms—thereby sharply reversing the decline of recent years—some $30 billion in external resources would be required during the 1984-1990 period for the region's GNP to grow at 4 percent.[7] The Kissinger commission on Central America estimated the cumulative net financing requirements of the region (including Panama) at $24 billion for the same period.[8] These inflows would permit per capita consumption to regain the levels of 1980 and, for some countries, those of the late 1970s. Presumably, even higher annual flows would be required to compensate for the region's poor economic performance in 1984-1985. Yet, the current outlook for external capital flows raises serious doubts as to whether the region's needs will be met.

Private Credit. The commercial banks have been concentrating on reducing their exposure in the region to the greatest extent possible, even to the point of cutting long-standing lines of revolving trade credits. For example, after the Nicaraguan revolution, the banks rescheduled their outstanding debts, but they have been unwilling to extend new credits and are now required by the U.S. banking authorities to set aside reserves against their Nicaraguan debts, on the assumption that they may never be fully repaid. After a period of freeze, the commercial banks agreed in early 1985 to provide Costa Rica with $75 million in new credits, as part of a stabilization program supported by the International Monetary Fund (IMF) and the World Bank. The Bretton Woods institutions warned the banks that the stabilization program could not proceed—and they would not lend—unless the banks contributed to the financing package. As an indication of their future intentions, the commercial banks proposed during the negotiations that they not be expected to provide additional credits in the future.[9] Even in 1985 the banks were due to receive much more from Costa Rica in interest payments—scheduled at $300-$400 million—than they were prepared to extend in new loans.

For the region as a whole, the international banking system is likely to be a net drain of capital, as interest payments continue to exceed any new lending. In order to at least partially reverse the banks' withdrawal, the Reagan administration has instructed the U.S. Export-Import Bank to provide Central America with $300 million in insurance and guarantees to stimulate short-term trade credits to the area. However, the banks will probably continue to view the region as one of high risk and low growth potential and will, therefore, remain squeamish.

Bilateral Donors. Bilateral donors have entered in the wake of the banks' withdrawal to become the region's most important source of external funding. The United States is now authorizing annual levels of economic aid of around $1 billion (see Table 4) and is by far the largest single donor for El Salvador, Honduras, and Costa Rica. Nicaragua has attracted a diverse range of donors in Western and Eastern Europe, the Middle East, and

TABLE 4. U.S. FOREIGN ASSISTANCE TO CENTRAL AMERICA, FY 1983-86(1)
(millions of $US)

	Economic Aid (2)				
	1983	1984	1984 (supplemental)	1985	1986 (request)
Belize	16.7	3.9	11.4	10.0	10.8
Costa Rica	212.4	107.5	66.2	201.8	187.4
El Salvador	241.9	212.4	113.3	310.7	350.6
Guatemala	26.6	16.0	16.6	73.0	77.0
Honduras	101.2	90.3	79.8	134.9	143.0
Panama	7.2	11.7	34.0	40.0	62.6
Regional programs	19.4	15.5	37.2	121.7	148.5
Central America Total	625.4	457.3	358.5	892.1	979.9

	Military Aid (3)				
	1983	1984	1984 (supplemental)	1985	1986 (request)
Belize	0.07	0.55	0.00	0.58	1.10
Costa Rica	2.63	2.13	7.00	9.20	2.73
El Salvador	81.30	64.80	131.75	128.30	132.60
Guatemala	0.00	0.00	0.00	0.30	10.30
Honduras	37.30	40.94	36.50	62.40	88.25
Panama	5.40	5.50	8.00	10.60	19.05
Regional programs	5.33	5.29	18.50	25.50	6.50
Central America Total	132.06	119.22	201.75	236.88	260.53

(1) In addition, State Department, Peace Corps, and USIA programs included in the Central American Initiative total $11.5 million (1984 supplemental), $86.6 million (1985), and $72.7 million (1986 request).

(2) Includes development assistance, economic support funds, and PL 480.

(3) Includes foreign military sales, Military Assistance Program & IMET.

Source: U.S. Department of State, Sustaining A Consistent Policy in Central America: One Year After the National Bipartisan Commission Report. Special Report no. 124, April 1985, Appendix C, p. 20.

Latin America who are providing $400–$500 million annually; on a per capita basis, Nicaragua has become the leading recipient of external resources flows.[10] The entire region has benefited from the subsidized sales of oil provided by Mexico and Venezuela under the San José Accords first signed in 1980.[11]

Although unforeseen political factors might intervene, at present no major net boost in bilateral flows seems likely. The Soviet Union and Eastern Europe might continue to increase their credit to Nicaragua, partly to compensate for declining flows from other bilateral sources. The European Economic Community has also pledged modest amounts of new monies for the region. These additional flows are unlikely to duplicate the impressive jumps in bilateral aid experienced in the recent past. Moreover, they will be at least partially offset by the less favorable terms being offered by the amended San José Accords, as Mexico and Venezuela—themselves hard-hit by falling oil prices and their own debt burdens—have reduced the margin of subsidy and become less tolerant of unpaid bills.

Multilateral Sources. The multilateral financial institutions have been approaching the region with caution. The Inter-American Development Bank authorized an annual average of about $335 million from 1980 to 1983 and plans to approve an annual average of $400 million from 1984 to 1986.[12] However, the World Bank and the IMF have preferred to concentrate their resources in South America and other parts of the Third World where political conditions have been less unstable, staff missions less exposed to physical danger, and governments more willing to adopt the recommended stabilization and adjustment programs. Thus, the World Bank has been authorizing an annual average of under $100 million in loans to Central America and has been inactive in El Salvador and Nicaragua.[13] Those stabilization programs that the IMF has agreed to support have often failed to live up to IMF standards, and have therefore been discontinued. However, in 1985, the IMF signed a standby agreement with Costa Rica that will provide $54 million, to be accompanied by a structural adjustment loan from the World Bank for $80 million. The Costa Rican example suggests that under the proper conditions, the Bretton Woods institutions could become important sources of additional finance for other

TABLE 5. GROSS DOMESTIC INVESTMENT BY DOLLARS
(millions of 1982 $US)

	1980	1981	1982	1983	1984
Costa Rica	1,111	692	516	644	737
El Salvador	483	465	417	383	399
Guatemala	1,118	1,273	1,042	850	830
Honduras	718	596	364	385	493
Nicaragua	396	612	506	550	459
Panama	933	1,051	976	784	N.A.
Total	4,759	4,689	3,821	3,596	

Source: IDB, Economic and Social Progress in Latin America. Washington, D.C.: IDB, 1985, p. 389.

countries of the region—once they attain a higher degree of political stability and are willing to accept the stricter conditions regarding economic reforms that accompany these larger outlays.

DOMESTIC SAVINGS AND INVESTMENT

The international economic environment is likely to continue to make life difficult for Central America. Medium-term prospects are further clouded by the sharp contraction in domestic investment and savings. As their deficits have widened, governments have become net dissavers and have been forced to slash capital expenditures. Private firms have seen their profits dwindle, and personal savings have shrunk as families attempt to maintain living standards in the face of falling real incomes. As a result, the region's net formation of fixed capital fell by 44 percent between 1979 and 1983 (see Table 5).[14] Not surprisingly, investment has fallen more drastically than GNP. The ability of nations to even maintain the existing capital stock and infrastructure—much less undertake new investments—has been impaired. In the struggle to place a floor under consumption levels, nations are sacrificing future productive capacity. Although it may be possible for governments to reduce their deficits and for some firms to become more profitable, societal pressures to allocate any additional resources to immediate consumption will be great. Thus, in Nicaragua—the one country that has maintained high investment levels—the government decided in early 1985 to sacrifice some programmed investments in favor of consumption, in order to slow the decline in living standards.[15]

THE POSTPONEMENT OF ECONOMIC STABILIZATION

THE ROLE OF GOVERNMENT

International economic and domestic political shocks have badly disrupted Central America's economic management. Historically, the region's powerful central banks had pursued conservative monetary policies that required governments to limit the size of their fiscal deficits. Moreover, governments tended to avoid large-scale foreign borrowing except when funds were available on highly concessional rates. But the crises of the 1970s caused Central American policymakers to set prudence aside and to run large external and internal deficits. The gap widened between foreign exchange earned through the exports of goods and services and what countries were spending on imports and debt service (the current account deficit), while government spending far outpaced revenues (the fiscal deficit).

The fiscal deficits resulted from the combination of increased government spending and declining revenues. As recession and political anxieties caused the private sector to retreat, governments stepped in to maintain employment and effective demand. Even those governments relatively unaccountable to public opinion felt the need to ease social pressures; for the first time in nearly two decades, in 1982 the Guatemalan government permitted real wages to rise significantly.[16] Governments also felt compelled to spend more on arms; by 1984 some 40 percent of the budgets of El Salvador and Nicaragua were being devoted to security.[17] At the same time, the decline in exports and imports adversely affected government budgets heavily dependent upon taxes on foreign trade, just as the general economic decline reduced the revenue garnered from taxes on domestic commerce and income.

TABLE 6. THE SIZE OF GOVERNMENT: CENTRAL GOVERNMENT EXPENDITURE AS PERCENTAGE OF GDP, 1979-1984 (1)

	1975	1979	1980	1981	1982	1983	1984
Guatemala	10.1	12.3	14.2	16.0	13.1	11.4	10.3
El Salvador	14.9	14.8	17.6	21.9	21.1	20.5	20.2
Honduras	18.9	18.6	22.9	21.5	23.8	23.0	26.3
Nicaragua	18.1	20.0	27.5	33.8	44.5	54.4	57.0
Costa Rica	15.6	19.2	20.0	18.1	17.1	20.4	21.8

(1) Includes current and capital expenditures (excluding amortization) plus net lending.

Source: World Bank and International Monetary Fund; data for 1975 is from Inter-American Development Bank, Economic and Social Progress in Latin America. Washington, D.C.: IDB, 1984, table 20, p. 431.

Increased governmental responsibilities combined with declining national production to yield an increase in the ratio of central government expenditures to GDP. In El Salvador, the central government's share of GDP rose from 15 percent in 1979 to 21 percent in 1983; the consolidated public sector, including state-owned firms and such decentralized agencies as social security, jumped from 27 percent to 39 percent (see Table 6). The Honduran and Costa Rican governments also increased their role, although less markedly. In Nicaragua, the demands of war reconstruction, renewed hostilities, the Sandinistas' populism, and the reticence of the private sector combined to push central government spending to over half of the total domestic production of goods and services. Guatemala has been the exception to this regionwide trend, as its ratio of spending to GDP at first rose but was then cut back by renewed efforts at fiscal austerity.

Governments struggled to raise taxes to cover at least a portion of their increased responsibilities. For example, Costa Rican taxes rose as a percentage of GDP from 12 percent in 1979 to 17 percent in 1983.[18] Nevertheless, regional efforts to boost government incomes were hampered by the low and

TABLE 7. CENTRAL GOVERNMENT OVERALL DEFICIT
AS A PERCENTAGE OF GDP, 1979-1984

	1975	1979	1980	1981	1982	1983	1984 (e)
El Salvador	1.8	N.A.	6.2	9.2	8.7	7.4	7.3
Guatemala	-0.9	2.6	4.7	7.4	4.7	3.6	3.6
Costa Rica	2.3	6.9	8.0	5.3	3.4	3.3	3.0
Nicaragua	5.9	6.8	10.3	10.1	18.3	24.4	23.2
Honduras	5.3	4.2	7.6	7.5	10.0	9.8	11.5

(e) = preliminary estimate

Sources: World Bank and International Monetary Fund; data for 1975 are from Inter-American Development Bank, *Economic and Social Progress in Latin America.* Washington, D.C.: IDB, 1984, Table 22, p. 432.

declining levels of national income, faulty tax collection systems, and in some cases strong sentiment—whether within the government or in key economic and political sectors—against taxation. The clash between the demands on government to spend and the inability to raise taxes proportionately inevitably generated a widening fiscal deficit. For the region as a whole, the average (unweighted) fiscal deficit as a percentage of GDP nearly doubled from 1979 to 1982, rising to 9 percent (see Table 7).

The fiscal deficits were caused, in part, by the decline in revenues from external trade. Fiscal deficits, in turn, caused further deterioration in the current account by increasing the demand for imports and by causing some products to be consumed at home that might have been sold abroad. Furthermore, as countries had to borrow to finance external deficits, rising interest payments on the accumulated debt added weight to the current account imbalance. For the region as a whole, current account deficits skyrocketed to slightly over $2 billion in 1981. These deficits were financed by a combination of massive external borrowing and the exhaustion of the region's foreign exchange reserves.

Predictably, fiscal deficits and foreign exchange shortages caused prices to rise. Although mild by South American standards, the jump in inflation rates to an average of 22 percent between 1980 and 1982 jolted a region that had enjoyed an unusual degree of price stability. Not accustomed to inflation, governments and some private firms failed to adjust some of their prices. Exchange rates became overvalued, and nominal interest rates became negative in real terms. The prices of some public-sector services—such as electricity or transportation—also tended to lag behind the inflation rate. The resulting subsidies placed further pressures on government budgets and printing presses.

GRADUALISM VERSUS "SHOCK TREATMENT"

In Central America, as throughout the Third World, societies have been debating whether "shock treatment" or more gradual reform is the least costly way to reduce their nations' external and internal imbalances.[19] Advocates of shock treatment argue that the sooner that accounts and prices are stabilized the sooner the economy will be freed from market distortions and the sooner the private sector will be willing to renew investment. Shock advocates also sometimes maintain that governments that act quickly have a better chance of imposing the necessary austerity measures before vested interests can organize an effective opposition. Moreover, a government that gives the appearance of having a strong program and direction will boost business confidence. Conversely, advocates of gradualism typically warn that shock treatments may result in an unnecessarily large loss of production and employment, typically hit the poor hardest, and may destabilize governments.

In earlier years, Central America's conservative regimes might have been expected to adopt orthodox, rapid stabilization programs. However, with some partial exceptions, governments in the 1980s opted for gradualism. This choice was dictated by the extreme social pressures on governments. It was financially feasible because external donors were willing to help finance the current accounts and fiscal deficits. In particular, Nicaragua, El Salvador, and Honduras have persistently run high fiscal deficits (see Table 7) and have barely begun to adjust their economies.*

Guatemala and Costa Rica have been partial exceptions to the gradualism approach. Guatemala never allowed its fiscal deficit to surpass 10 percent of GDP, and it began in 1982 to cut fiscal expenditures and imports; further downward adjustments occurred in 1985 as the government continued to seek a reduction of the fiscal deficit. Even more dramatic has been the Costa Rican story. After postponing stabilization through massive borrowing from commercial banks between 1978 and 1981, Costa Rica slammed on the brakes in 1982. The fiscal deficit was sharply narrowed by cutting subsidies and the real wages of government employees, increasing taxes, and raising the prices of government-provided services. The current account deficit also narrowed as imports fell from $1.2 billion to under $900 million.[20]

Several factors account for the more austere policies adopted by Guatemala and Costa Rica. Both governments felt more politically able to implement stabilization programs than did the other governments in the region. Guatemala's military rulers faced a nascent guerrilla challenge and a weak urban political or union movement that could be controlled or repressed. Costa Rica, in contrast, was able to rely on its reservoir of democratic legitimacy to manage the strains produced by austerity. Moreover, both governments faced severe external financial constraints that compelled drastic action. Guatemala's poor international image limited access to large-scale assistance from the United States and other bilateral donors. In 1981, Costa Rica had not yet begun to receive large amounts of U.S. aid, and the country's main funders—the commercial banks—had suddenly judged the nation uncreditworthy. Interestingly, when U.S. aid flows began to swell, Costa Rica reverted to a more gradualist approach to stabilization as its trade and current account deficits widened in 1983-1984.[21]

---

*Subsequent to this writing, in January 1986 the government of El Salvador announced a reform package that included a currency devaluation and the raising of the prices of some public services, including transportation.

Central American governments have also moved slowly to adjust the prices of their currency (the exchange rate) and internal savings (the interest rate). Fearing that large devaluations would provoke internal inflation, governments have preferred to devalue gradually by adopting multiple exchange-rate systems. Some imports have continued to enter at the old, "official" rate, while an increasing number of imports enter at the less favorable, new "parallel" rate. In some cases, governments have established a complex system of differentiated rates for different categories of products. In addition, governments have sometimes permitted a free or black market. These multiple exchange-rate regimes have typically been accompanied by higher tariff barriers, official licensing of imports, and other trade restrictions, as well as foreign exchange rationing and other controls over capital movements.[22]

Traditionally, the IMF has objected to such multiple exchange-rate regimes on the grounds that they introduce price distortions and bureaucratic inefficiencies. Moreover, the slow pace of the devaluation amounts to a disincentive to those exporters not benefiting from the higher exchange rates. However, since multiple exchange-rate regimes have become so common in developing countries during the recent crisis, the IMF has tended to tolerate them, while pushing countries to speed the process of full devaluation and the return to a single, unified exchange rate.

Central American governments have also moved slowly to adjust interest rates to inflation rates. Governments have tended to set various rates, some still below the rate of inflation. The IMF has traditionally viewed negative nominal interest rates as being disincentives to savers and as resulting in inefficient allocation of investment funds. Central American governments have worried that high interest rates would add to inflation and would mortally wound already seriously ill businesses.

The IMF has frequently been frustrated in Central America because governments have hesitated to implement tough austerity measures and have been able to avoid doing so because other external donors—notably the United States—have been willing to fund gradualist approaches. Balance-of-payments support is fungible, so it is often difficult to judge the ultimate use of funds. Nevertheless, government officials in the region believe that external aid has helped them cover budget deficits, meet external debt service, and increase imports both for consumer goods and inputs into industry and agriculture. In effect, large-scale external aid enables governments to spend without increasing taxes, to narrow the balance-of-payments deficit without devaluation, and to increase the availability of investment funds without raising domestic interest rates. The U.S. Agency for International Development (AID) is aware of these dangers and increasingly has been pursuing "policy dialogues" with Central American governments that have included an occasional freezing of funds pending adoption of recommended reforms.[23] But AID faces the dilemma of having to balance two sometimes conflicting goals: to meet the political objectives of propping up a regime while simultaneously advocating economic measures that, in the short run, can be politically destabilizing. AID's leverage is, therefore, less than that of the IMF, which has been more willing to walk away from nonperforming Central American governments.

The gradualist approach has been politically expedient for Central American governments. Has it been economically effective, in the sense of minimizing the costs and laying the groundwork for economic recovery? Unfortunately, more country studies will be needed before definitive judgments can be made. In order to determine the realistic range of options that were available,[24] such studies will have to consider carefully both the political constraints as well as the economic objectives that governments faced. However, one can tentatively note that the nation that adopted the most strenuous stabilization approach in 1981-1982 registered the best growth rates in 1983-1984; but the very political factors that permitted Costa Rica to take decisive stabilization measures have sheltered it from the political turmoil that has shocked the rest of the region. Elsewhere, in the absence of a political environment that would have permitted a renewal of business confidence, more rapid stabilization programs may have gone unrewarded.

More study is also needed in order to determine the distribution of the burden of austerity within each society. Some observers believe that the urban lower-middle and middle classes have been suffering disproportionately because their living standards have been hard hit by inflation and wage freezes. The urban population also may have been disadvantaged by devaluations because they consume more imported products than the peasantry does. Moreover, the peasantry can more readily fall back on subsistence farming, artisanry, and their extended families. Finally, the urban poor have suffered from cuts in social spending, high food prices, and unemployment. In any case, hard data are lacking.

Realities also differ among countries. In San Salvador and Guatemala City, the visibility of Mercedes Benzes, videocassette recorders, and other luxury imports suggests that the upper classes have been able to defend themselves, and some may have even benefited from the opportunities for speculation in currency, real estate, and commerce. In Managua, in contrast, urban consumers have been constrained by severe currency and import controls and by graded income, wealth, and consumer taxes that hit the wealthy hard. However, a more complete picture of the impact of government policies on incomes in Nicaragua would also have to consider the many effects of fierce inflation and badly overvalued exchange rates—the results, in part, of the government's decision to protect the average consumer and to postpone stabilization.[25]

STRUCTURAL ADJUSTMENT IN THE FUTURE

The stabilization process is still incomplete in Central America. Indeed, the region seems destined to experience a period of prolonged austerity. Nevertheless, it is not too early to ponder strategies for future development. Despite the preoccupations with managing immediate stabilization programs and obtaining security objectives, many Central Americans and foreign observers are already beginning to devise development plans for the region's eventual economic recovery and growth. Just as, in 1944, in the midst of World War II, the conference held at Bretton Woods, New Hampshire, laid the basis for the structure of the postwar global economy, so it is possible today to conceive of programs that will be implemented once financial stabilization is achieved and political conflict subsides in Central America.

The depth of the region's crisis has stimulated intense criticism of the development model that held sway during the 1960s and 1970s. The model that combined traditional agricultural exports with an industrialization process oriented toward regional markets has been found wanting by nearly all political sectors. Enthusiasm for traditional agricultural exports has been dampened by adverse conditions on international markets. The process of industrialization behind high tariff walls has been criticized by conservatives, among others, for its interventionism and inefficiencies;[26] by the center for its tilt away from agriculture and for its other inequities;[27] and by the left for its dependence on foreign inputs and for its low labor absorption rates.[28] All agree that the strategy needs dramatic revision.

Throughout Central America, the debate over long-term economic strategies is less polarized than the conflicts over political models. For example, no major groups are advocating autarky at either the national or regional levels. All recognize that Central America—with its approximately 22 million people and gross product of only about $20 billion—must remain integrated into the international economy. National preferences differ somewhat regarding the appropriate trading strategy, particularly with respect to product and market emphases; but these differences tend to reflect existing productive capacities and potential comparative advantage rather than ideological predilections.

Discussions regarding future growth strategies focus on five potential sources of growth: traditional agricultural exports; agroindustry; transformation industries (export-oriented light manufactures); industrial production for a revived Central American Common Market; and the production of basic grains and other essential items for domestic consumption. In the 1980s, the depressed state of regional and domestic markets and pressing foreign exchange needs have focused attention throughout the region on the first three categories of exports targeted at international markets.

TRADITIONAL AGRICULTURAL EXPORTS

Historically, the economies of Central America have done well when basic agricultural exports have thrived. During the

1960s and early 1970s, rising revenues from coffee, cotton, bananas, sugar, and meat provided the capital for industrialization and rising consumption. A dynamic, traditional export agriculture proved to be compatible with—and even a precondition for—progress in other sectors.

The region's current economic misfortunes are substantially a result of weak international prices, but they can also be attributed to a decline in production of some export crops, particularly cotton. In addition, Nicaragua, Guatemala, and Honduras have underutilized or let lie fallow lands where cultivation of traditional export crops could be substantially augmented. For example, AID estimated that Guatemala's traditional agricultural exports could grow by $445 million between 1984 and 1989, accounting for half of Guatemala's total projected export expansion.[29] The Nicaraguan government estimated that the volume of exported cotton will rise by 48 percent between 1983 and 1987, and sugar exports will increase by 79 percent.[30] Costa Rica presents a partial exception, in that traditional agricultural production has not fallen dramatically and there are not large tracts of fallow land waiting to be colonized.

But throughout most of the region, traditional agricultural exports seem to offer good opportunities for relatively rapid growth in the short to medium term. This option, however, does run the risk of restricting diversification efforts and further linking economies to the rise and fall of commodity prices on international markets.

AGROINDUSTRY

Agroindustry has emerged as the exciting new sector for long-term growth. The Costa Rican Ministry of Planning has proposed to "convert the agricultural sector into the central pivot of Costa Rican economic development in the coming years. It begins with the strategy of returning to the land, with the understanding that the national development potential lies in the transformation of agricultural products rather than of imported inputs. . . . "[31] Jaime Wheelock, Nicaraguan minister of agriculture, has expressed similar aspirations for his nation: "Nicaragua is not a financial center, nor do we have industry, large commercial installations, or oil. What then do we possess? Natural resources—so that our entire economic strategy is based in the industrial potential of our natural resources."[32]

The new attention to agroindustry arises from a favorable reading of its international marketing potential, as well as from the belief that the existing industrial plant—constructed to supply the regional market—is an artificial transplant requiring a high component of imported inputs. An industrial plant based on the region's comparative advantage in agriculture and better integrated, through backward linkages, into the national economy would be more competitive; it would also be a more efficient net generator of foreign exchange. It might also create more employment. Some of the prospective crops—including vegetables and fruits—are labor intensive, and the vertically integrated procedures of processing and marketing would absorb additional manpower. The intention is to transform cotton into clothes, sugar into candy and perhaps gasohol, and wood into furniture.

Despite its natural potential, agroindustry faces several obstacles. Being a relatively new line of development, it will require fresh capital at a time when investors hesitate to take risks because of the unsettled political climate. Foreign investors, whose participation is important for organizing the processing procedures and for gaining entry into global markets, are particularly wary. Moreover, access to markets in industrial countries has traditionally been impeded by graded tariff structures that protect their domestic processing plants. The Caribbean Basin Initiative removed some of these barriers, but Central American manufacturers complain that U.S. manufacturing or commercial firms will continue to use their oligopolistic powers to restrain the entrance of some Central American products, such as instant coffee. Finally, even if these obstacles can be overcome, the impact on national economies will generally be limited in the near future. Starting at a low base, agroindustrial exports will remain small in absolute terms; for example, AID estimates that if Guatemala's nontraditional exports increase by a solid 10 percent per year between 1984 and 1989, they will only rise by $105 million, to $275 million, and account for 14 percent of total exports.[33]

TRANSFORMATION INDUSTRIES (EXPORT-ORIENTED LIGHT MANUFACTURES)

An alternative approach to industrial exports is the *maquila* or transformation industries. Rather than seeking integration into the national economy, transformation industries are established as enclaves that use cheap labor to add value to goods whose inputs come from abroad and whose final markets are located overseas. These labor-intensive, light manufacturing processes typically involve transnational corporations and include electronics, toys, sporting goods, and textiles. The host nation benefits because both employment and foreign exchange earnings increase.

Prior to its political crisis, El Salvador had begun to establish transformation industries in such "free trade zones" as San Bartolo. The nation's limited land resources and high population density made industrialization a necessity; and its reputation for a low-wage, high-productivity labor force attracted foreign investors. Since then, real wages have fallen even further, and the CBI has facilitated access to the U.S. market. Significant new investments, however, will await a more tranquil political climate.

Maquilas have been heavily criticized for employing primarily young women, for being separate from the host economy, and for being ready to pull up stakes at the slightest disturbance. For these reasons, Central Americans now tend to see *maquilas* not as engines of growth but rather as useful complements to other strategies.

INDUSTRIAL PRODUCTION: A REVIVED CENTRAL AMERICAN COMMON MARKET

A cloud of pessimism has descended over the Central American Common Market. As a result of declining incomes, intraregional trade (mostly in industrial products) fell from nearly $1.1 billion Central American pesos in 1980 to $700 million pesos in 1984 (see Table 8). Foreign exchange pressures have resulted in new intraregional tariffs and other trade restrictions and in "beggar-thy-neighbor" devaluations. Even prior to the current crisis, many in the region were questioning the viability of an industrial base oriented toward a relatively small market

TABLE 8. CENTRAL AMERICAN COMMON MARKET EXPORTS,
1980-1984
(millions of Central American pesos)

	GUATEMALA	HONDURAS	EL SALVADOR	COSTA RICA	NICARAGUA	TOTAL
1980	403.7	83.9	295.8	270.3	75.4	1,129.1
1981	355.5	65.9	206.5	238.0	70.9	936.8
1982	320.1	51.9	174.2	167.2	52.1	765.5
1983	308.7	61.3	164.9	198.2	33.5	766.6
1984	291.4	49.4	157.2	171.8	37.1	706.9

Source: "Macroeconomic statistics of Central America," Secretaria Permanente del Tratado General de Integracion Economica Centroamericana, Guatemala City, June 1985, p. 31.

and apparently without the capacity to sell outside the region. The increasing divergence of Central American political systems and economic performances has raised further doubts about the Common Market's future. Even those who see the Common Market as an essential base for Central American industry see little prospects for a near-term revival of the region's effective purchasing power. The Common Market can only be the sum of its parts, and depressed income levels in each nation limit the demand for traded goods. All five nations, therefore, are seeking to diversify their markets and products, which means even if the Common Market recovers, its importance will be diminished.

Interest in rejuvenating the Common Market varies throughout the region. Reflecting their industries' considerable stake in the region's markets, Guatemalans and Costa Ricans are the most interested in the Common Market's future, although Costa Rica is annoyed at the inability of its regional trading partners to cancel some $250 million in accumulated debts. El Salvador and Nicaragua are preoccupied with internal political problems. Honduras is the most indifferent, having withdrawn from the CACM over a decade ago to seek more protection through bilateral agreements.

Nevertheless, the ancient aspiration for regional integration dies slowly. It is not yet politically acceptable to publicly reject the Common Market concept. Moreover, government officials continue to deflect pressures by external donors to take actions that would undermine the CACM. In 1984, Costa Rica reportedly resisted efforts by staff of the World Bank to condition a loan on tariff cuts that would have violated the region's external tariff agreement-the central instrument of the Common Market. Despite current political strains, the five nations have continued to cooperate in many economic matters, including the joint presentation of a program of economic recovery to external donors.[34] Substantial progress has also been made toward establishing a new common external tariff regime.

The logic that led to the creation of the Common Market remains valid. During the 1960s and the 1970s the CACM was an important engine of growth for the region's fledgling manufacturing sector, as firms took advantage of an enlarged regional market protected against competition from external producers. The CACM allows for economies of scale in production, the saving of foreign exchange via the substitution of regional products for imports, and a more attractive market for foreign investors. Increased regional trade also has served the political objective of enhanced contacts among the region's businessmen, bureaucrats, and economists.

If the Common Market is to recover, several reforms will be required.

Tariff Reform. The common external tariff needs an overhaul. Tariff reform could make Central American firms more efficient and more competitive, by replacing a confusing product classification system with an internationally accepted one and by exposing some firmsto greater foreign competition. Negotiators from the four member countries have agreed on a new tariff convention and have created a special body, the Council on Tariffs, to oversee the new regulations. The new system would set a maximum tariff rate of 100 percent, thereby reducing the breadth of dispersion among rates, and would simplify the tariff codes by eliminating many special exemptions. In particular, in order to foster more integrated industries, tariffs would be lowered on final goods while raised for some raw materials and other inputs that could be locally produced. The new convention would also seek to make the system more transparent by separating protective tariffs from consumption taxes on traded goods. These reforms suggest both a commitment to the Common Market as well as the widespread of recognition of the need to reduce and simplify some tariffs. But it is too early to determine what the impact of these reforms will be, and there are already misgivings being voiced as to their immediate effect. Until now, many Common Market industries had been exempt from paying any tariffs at all and the new reforms though lowering tariff rates will eliminate these exemptions. Thus, the reforms may actually be counterproductive to trade incentives. Other criticisms come from free trade advocates who believe that the Common Market itself is a flawed concept or those who favor rapid and drastic tariff cuts.

Improved Liquidity. Intraregional liquidity needs to be increased. The Central American clearinghouse (Camara de Compensacion) was created to facilitate intraregional trade, but the large deficits accumulated by Nicaragua and El Salvador have exceeded its capacity. As a result, Costa Rica is no longer willing to extend new trade credits to its neighbors.

The Kissinger commission recommended that external donors help the Camara to cancel existing credits. However, the region's very uneven growth rates could result in a rapid resurgence of new imbalances. In any event, the Reagan administration presumably is opposed to an action that would benefit Nicaragua (as a debtor nation).

Balance of Trade. The structural trade imbalances in the region need to be addressed. Disparate fiscal and monetary policies being pursued in the region have produced trade imbalances and large debits. Nations could seek greater harmonization of fiscal and monetary policies, although Nicaragua currently opposes this solution. More flexible exchange rate regimes present an alternative path to more stable trading relations. A third, less efficient, but perhaps more politically feasible approach at this time would be the establish ment of a series of bilateral deals that would assure balanced trade.

Recapitalizing CABEI. The Central American Bank for Economic Integration badly needs refinancing. Limited capital and a significant buildup of arrears by its Central American clients have sharply restricted the region's own development institution. In order to allow for a loan program of $300 million a year over the next decade, the Bank's management has requested capital contributions of $50 million from each Central American nation and $666.6 million from extraregional sources.[35]

The CACM has suffered from the perception that the stronger countries with more efficient industries have benefited disproportionately. One way to address this imbalance is to design projects that involve more than one country and that bring large benefits to the weaker nations. Such integration projects might be proposed as part of a larger regionwide agreement that would set national and regional investment priorities. A strengthened CABEI could play a key role in designing and financing such a plan.

Reforming the common external tariff, refinancing the clearinghouse, addressing the structural trade imbalances, and recapitalizing CABEI present a formidable but not insurmountable agenda. However, the problem of Nicaragua remains. Theoretically, it should not be impossible to devise trading arrangements between a country with strong government intervention in its economy and neighboring states that are more market oriented. Indeed, Nicaraguan economic ministers continue to participate actively in CACM affairs, although other governments have grown skeptical of Nicaragua's financial ability to live up to its agreements. The greater danger to the Common Market may come from the United States, which tends to oppose any initiatives that might benefit Nicaragua. In commenting on AID's own preliminary strategy for strengthening the CACM, which is based on the positive recommendations of the Kissinger commission, the AID mission in Honduras has noted: "As a practical matter, we believe that the issue of excluding Nicaragua as a beneficiary country may prove to be an insurmountable stumbling block to negotiating the proposed policy reforms and to implementation of the proposed programs."[36]

THE PRODUCTION OF BASIC GRAINS AND ESSENTIALS FOR THE DOMESTIC MARKET

Pressures to increase exports have diverted attention from local markets. Nevertheless, the combination of foreign exchange shortages and devaluations should eventually stimulate further import substitution, once effective demand begins to recover. The informal sector has already been filling the vacuum left by the disappearance of imported commodities, but large-scale producers—like the CACM industries—will continue to operate below capacity until imported inputs are more readily available and consumers have more cash. The domestic market can provide a quick kick to business—as it did to Costa Rica in 1984—but only so long as the foreign exchange bottleneck is relaxed.

More immediate gains are possible in agriculture. The development strategy of CACM industries and export agriculture pursued in the 1960s and 1970s neglected the farmer who cultivated basic grains for domestic consumption, and food imports rose in the 1970s. In the 1980s, the production of basic grains (beans, corn, and rice) has benefited from the spontaneous decisions of farmers in conflictive zones to return to subsistence crops and in some cases, from deliberate government policy. For example, Nicaraguan production of basic grains rose by one-third from the 1980-1981 to the 1983-1984 seasons.[37] An increase in basic grain production would save foreign exchange, improve income distribution, and could increase demand for locally made industrial products.

Each country will select a somewhat different mix of these five sectors to form its development strategy. Natural endowments and comparative advantage, as well as opportunities offered by international markets, will probably weigh more than politics. Thus, El Salvador may well emphasize traditional agricultural exports, the Central American Common Market, and transformation industries. Nicaragua will probably look to traditional agricultural exports, agroindustry, and basic grains. Costa Rica may emphasize agroindustry and the *maquilas*. The political debate will center more on instruments than on ends, and on the distribution of the fruits of growth: Opinions today in Central America differ most sharply on the relative roles that government and the market should play, and over the degrees of inequality that are politically or morally tolerable.

3
Economic Growth and Political Order
Bruce M. Bagley

Central America's turbulent political history during the high growth decades of the 1950s and 1960s tragically confirms the proposition that rapid economic expansion does not necessarily or automatically produce political stability, much less viable democratic regimes. Indeed, of the five Central American republics, only Costa Rica was able to combine rapid growth with democratic stability during this period. In stark contrast, the experiences of Nicaragua, El Salvador, and Guatemala grimly demonstrated that accelerated growth is often fundamentally disruptive of the traditional social and political order and frequently results in harsh authoritarianism. The inability of the region's traditional regimes to incorporate the new social forces brought into being by rapid economic growth—and thereby to institutionalize stable and legitimate political systems—lies at the heart of the current political-military conflicts in the region. Economic reactivations in the absence of major internal political and economic reforms will not resolve the political legitimacy crises that now beset several countries in the region. Conversely, failure to generate growth could result in growing political polarization and, eventually, political breakdown, even in relatively stable nations such as Costa Rica and Honduras.

Any discussion of alternative economic development strategies in Central America must inevitably deal with the underlying questions concerning the political framework within which economic growth is to take place. Two basic issues are central to this debate. Who (which groups, classes, sectors of society) will direct the development process? And who will receive the benefits of development?

ALTERNATIVE POLITICAL ECONOMIES

A concatenation of popular pressures, economic failures, and foreign influences—different in each nation—has reversed the pattern of overt military rule predominant in the region in recent decades. Indeed, each country now lays claim to "democracy" as the operative regime type or, as in the case of Guatemala, is engaged in a process of "democratization." Despite their use of the term *democracy*, however, the internal structures and dynamics of these regimes—and thus the beneficiaries of future economic development—may vary significantly.

At least three distinct models or ideal-types of democracy, each with its own underlying political economy paradigm, have been articulated in the region. From the right, for example, emerges a vision of "democracy-with-liberty," premised on formal democratic procedures, minimal state intervention in the free market (laissez-faire), and a "trickle-down" approach to development and equity issues. The radical left, in contrast, advocates a "revolutionary" version of democracy rooted in an ideology of popular power, active state intervention in the economy, a mixed-economy model with extensive state ownership, and radical redistributive reforms to reduce socioeconomic inequalities among social classes. Eschewing both of these extremes, moderates or centrists embrace a "democracy-with-justice" model anchored in Social and Christian Democratic traditions of participatory democracy, selective state intervention ("industrial policy" involving active state regulation but not large-scale involvement in productive processes or state ownership), and mild distributive (rather than redistributive) reforms to improve living standards among the lowest income groups in society.

These three political economy models constitute ideal-types and thus are not found in pure form anywhere in the region. Moreover, there are not always sharp divisions between the constructs; rather, they exist on a continuum. Some individuals, for example, would probably place themselves somewhere between laissez-faire and industrial policy, and some might consider industrial policy to be a realistic model for the 1980s but something more akin to laissez-faire to be a desirable objective. The purpose of these ideal-types is heuristic; they are designed to help clarify the nature of the elite consensus (or pact of domination) upon which each model rests, the type of political regime or system proposed, and the economic policies most closely associated with each.

DEMOCRACY-WITH-LIBERTY

In this model, democratic liberty is synonymous with freedom of the marketplace. The role of the state is understood to be limited, confined essentially to maintaining internal order and guaranteeing the conditions for private capital accumulation. The relative autonomy of the state would be carefully circumscribed, government involvement in the productive sector severely curtailed, and state welfare functions kept to a minimum. Political control would be exercised by a center-right coalition made up of the traditional landowning classes (involved in agroexport activities), the urban capitalist class (engaged in finance, industry, and commerce), and allied segments of the urban and rural middle classes. Mass political participation would remain carefully channeled and controlled.[38]

The political economy paradigm underlying this "pure" conservative view of the state is a modern-day laissez-faire or "supply-side" model. The decline of the CACM, the growth of government, and the resurgence of free-market thinking in the United States and some Western European countries have increased the influence of what Central Americans call the neoliberal school. Beyond repeating the neoclassical arguments that are widespread in U.S. academic circles and the Bretton Woods institutions on behalf of "getting prices right," the Central American proponents of this model make the case that their small, open economies are "price-takers" and must accept the global economy as they find it: Domestic prices should be brought into line with international prices in order to encourage efficient operations.[39]

The neoliberals would sharply cut back on state interventionism.[40] They believe prices—including interest rates and exchange rates—should be deregulated and other price controls abandoned. Taxes that distort the prices of labor or capital or discourage savings should be eliminated, perhaps in favor of a value-added tax. The size of government as a percentage of GNP should be limited, and parastatals sold off. Most importantly, tariffs should be quickly and sharply reduced to a uniform rate of perhaps 10 percent. (Temporary subsidies might be allowed to firms that lose their protectionism, and additional external financing might be sought to ease the transition.) The neoliberal tariff policy might well mean the effective termination of the CACM. Neoliberals tend to see Central American economies as essentially competitive among themselves and consider that the global economy offers much greater opportunities.[41]

Although the neoliberal view has gained some strength recently in Central America, it still remains a minority view in academia, and most businesspeople and politicians (at least in practice if not in rhetoric) still prefer a more activist state. For example, despite the entrenched power of right-wing political groups, contemporary El Salvador does not fit the democracy-with-liberty ideal-type in a number of key respects. At least since the 1960s, the Salvadoran state has played an interventionist role in guiding the national economy. The five-year-old civil war has further distorted the pure democracy-with-liberty model by enlarging the role of the military in the political economy of the country and obliging the state and the private sector to underwrite expensive counterinsurgency activities. Since 1981, U.S. military assistance has defrayed most of these costs (see Table 4), but the remaining budgetary burden has been substantial. The agrarian, marketing, and banking reforms introduced in late 1979 by the first civilian-military junta also represent deviations from the neoliberal ideal-type. Finally, the mildly populist proclivities of President Jose Napoleon Duarte and his Christian Democratic party have resulted in the state assuming additional welfare functions. The Salvadoran right appears confident that it will be able to control Duarte and dilute his reformist zeal while gradually implementing a model that more closely approximates the democracy-with-liberty ideal-type.[42]

Although it has been ruled by the political right and the military for decades, Guatemala has also failed to adopt a democracy-with-liberty model or its underlying neoliberal economic paradigm. At the political level, the Guatemalan military has been reluctant to accept even formal democracy as a result of fears of a leftist triumph at the polls. At the economic level, the Guatemalan state has been actively interventionist and the armed forces have required rising budgetary outlays to combat domestic insurgencies and preserve political control.[43]

Although any political faction with neoliberal economic views that gains power can expect to find support and encouragement from external donors, particularly the Reagan administration, many observers question the long-term political viability of the democracy-with-liberty model. The most basic criticism is that this model simply does not have the capacity to generate the popular legitimacy essential to the successful consolidation of a stable civilian regime. The economic sacrifices demanded from the lower classes by this approach frequently must be exacted through authoritarian measures and thus militate against institutionalization of any form of democratic regime. In addition, even conservative Salvadoran and Guatemalan businessmen consistently resist the loss of state protection contemplated in the model's economic strategy. Because of this basic tension or contradiction between democratic participation and neoliberal economic policies, no Central American country is actually attempting to implement a pure democracy-with-liberty model at present and none is likely to undertake such a project in the foreseeable future.

DEMOCRACY-WITH-JUSTICE

In this second model, democratic justice translates into relatively broad-based political participation in the system and extensive socioeconomic reform. The role of the state is more interventionist, designed to ensure not only the conditions for private capital accumulation but also a much greater degree of equity. State welfare (distributive) activities are extensive and viewed as legitimate. The ruling coalition is centrist, dominated by the urban capitalist class, with political allies in the urban and rural middle classes and support groups in organized labor and the peasantry. The political right (especially the traditional large landowners) is necessarily small and politically weak.[44]

The economic paradigm underlying this democracy-with-justice model is an industrial-policy approach. The neoliberal view is radical in the Central American context; more precisely, it restates the pre–World War II liberalism that held sway when Central America was a commodity exporter with very weak governments. More centrist or reformist is the industrial-policy approach that recognizes that the CACM needs modernizing and that governmental bureaucracies need rationalizing, but which would dismantle neither.[45] Market mechanisms are often efficient, but business-government cooperation is sometimes necessary to compete globally or to attain social welfare goals.

Industrial-policy advocates justify state activism on grounds that the market will fail to allocate resources in nationally optimal ways.[46] The market will not build the necessary physical infrastructure—roads, ports, storage facilities—nor invest enough in human capital—schools, worker training programs. Moreover, in the small Central American economies, oligopolistic industrial structures will inevitably produce inefficient market solutions. In particular, private banks will be tied to families or industrial groups. Industrial-policy advocates also consider that Central American industrialization is too incipient to be able to take off and compete internationally if left to the mercy of the market. Governments must aid infant industries and other firms as they adopt new technologies and seek to enter new markets; the *dirigiste* examples of France and Japan are the models—or nineteenth-century American mercantilism.

Industrial-policy proponents seek a gradual reduction and simplification of the CACM's common external tariff, along the lines currently being negotiated. Central American industries should be subjected to the winds of international competition but not blown away by overexposure. Moreover, governments should actively seek to aid firms—whether serving the domestic, regional, or international markets—through a battery of instruments, including tax breaks, tariff exemptions, and credit subsidies. The full range of government policies should be reviewed to guarantee consistency with industrial policies. Similarly, parastatals should be given a hard look to determine if they should be sold off or put on a firmer financial footing.

Although generally more disposed to larger government— and to closing existing fiscal deficits through higher taxation rather than expenditure reductions—than neoliberals, industrial-policy advocates' attitudes toward taxation vary by country. Costa Ricans generally feel that the ratio of taxes to GNP is already adequate; Guatemalans and Salvadorans are more likely to believe that higher levels of taxation will be required if the government is to have the necessary resources to cover its economic and social obligations. Some industrial-policy adherents would also use the tax system to pursue equity objectives, preferring direct taxes on income and wealth to indirect taxes on essential consumer items.[47]

This school of thought generally considers the CACM to be compatible with an export promotion strategy aimed at third markets. Indeed, production for regional and international markets can be not only compatible but self-reinforcing. A firm can better compete on the international market and sell at lower marginal cost if it can readily sell to a regional, captive market at average cost. Moreover, the experience and capital that the firm acquires serving regional buyers will assist it in penetrating foreign markets. In addition, international trade can have a positive benefit for the Common Market by increasing income levels and purchasing power.[48]

Costa Rica constitutes the archetype of the democracy-with-justice model. The Reagan administration, like the Carter administration before it, has generally been supportive of Costa Rican-style democracy, as have most other external donors. In the face of a severe crisis in the first half of the 1980s, however, the interventionist role of the Costa Rican state in the national economy, especially its broad welfare functions, has come under intense criticism from U.S.AID, IMF, and World Bank officials, and external pressure to reduce these activities has mounted steadily. Costa Rica's financial needs have increased the leverage of creditors, who seek to form alliances with like-minded domestic businessmen, technocrats, and politicians.

The imperative to compress social spending and real wages poses a fundamental dilemma for Costa Rica's leadership, for it threatens to erode the basis upon which the regime's stability rests. The legitimacy of the democracy-with-justice model is grounded in its ability to provide social justice; welfare benefits are a key instrument in this process. If income levels fail to recover in Costa Rica, rising social and political tensions may ensue and could ultimately produce regime breakdown. Following more than five years of economic contraction, Costa Rican society has remained remarkably stable; nevertheless, the state's deepening fiscal crisis, intensifying fears of Sandinista subversion, and continuing U.S. pressures could catalyze a shift of power to the right and away from the democracy-with-justice model.[49]

Honduras, the poorest country in Central America, returned to civilian, democratic rule in 1982 after more than a decade of military governments. Former Liberal President Roberto Suazo Cordova campaigned on a democracy-with-justice platform. In practice, however, the international economic recession and low prices for the country's major agricultural exports have combined to undercut the government's ability to finance the promised reforms. The Honduran military, bolstered by substantial increases in U.S. military assistance, has remained a major economic and political force in the country. President Suazo's reformist political project was further undermined by widespread cronyism and corruption in his government.

Military distaste for the messy aspects of civilian rule in Honduras is palpable. If social and political tensions continue to rise and the civilian leadership proves unable to manage them, the military might be tempted to return to power. However, the Reagan administration favors the preservation of civilian rule and would actively discourage a military coup; thus, civilian rule is likely, although not guaranteed, to endure in some form. If the border conflict between Nicaragua and Honduras erupts into a hotter war, the military may well assume expanded powers, with both domestic civilian and U.S. acquiescence.[50]

Even though the democracy-with-justice model clearly confronts serious political problems, at the economic level some variant of industrial policy seems most likely to prevail in Central America. It represents the least radical departure from existing rules, and, therefore, would upset fewer vested interests. Moreover, it avoids the essential weakness in the other two approaches: a dogmatic faith in either the market or the government. In fact, U.S.AID itself—rhetoric aside—tends to favor not laissez-faire but a positive, government-supported policy for export promotion; and in early 1985 even the Sandinistas implemented major reforms to give greater scope to market mechanisms.

REVOLUTIONARY DEMOCRACY

The Sandinista regime in Nicaragua also lays claim to democratic credentials. In this revolutionary model, democracy is understood to involve a fundamental reordering of class relationships within society. The state is viewed as a key instrument in the process of societal reorganization, and its role is pervasive. Integral to the revolutionary political project is the partial redistribution of property, wealth, and consumption away from the traditionally dominant landowning, agroexporting, and urban capitalist classes to workers, peasants, and the urban poor. Political power is the province of the revolutionary leadership or vanguard. The private sector and limited opposition activity are permitted as long as they do not threaten the revolutionary coalition's political control.[51]

Even though socialist economic models take many forms, all generally emphasize the role of the state in the ownership and control of the "commanding heights" of an economy and see government as the chief engine for capital accumulation and investment. Socialism is compatible with an active private sector, especially in small firms and commerce. In the Nicaraguan case, large farms and industries remain in private hands, but the government attempts to influence private decisions through its control of foreign exchange, bank credit, taxation, and other fiscal incentives.[52] A private sector is encouraged for several reasons in Nicaragua: The Sandinista Front for National Liberation (FSLN) recognizes the limited managerial capacity of the state; some Sandinistas see a private sector as an important component of their project of political pluralism; and international actors are conditioning their policies toward Nicaragua on the private sector's survival.[53]

In Nicaragua, some leading thinkers recognize the limits on socialism that result from Nicaragua being a small economy on the periphery of the capitalist system.[54] Accumulation must occur not through heavy industry but through traditional export crops (albeit with a higher level of value added through processing). By socializing some land and by marketing agricultural exports, the state can capture the rent generated by Nicaragua's comparative advantage. The state, however, must run a cautious fiscal and monetary policy; in a small, open economy, an overly expansionist fiscal policy quickly runs up against a foreign exchange bottleneck.

Because of their concern for equity, socialists in the Central American context may advocate turning the internal terms of trade in favor of the many small farmers. They may also advocate holding down the wages of workers in the more technically advanced firms, both to increase the profits generated in that sector as well as to hold down overall wage levels so as to increase labor-capital ratios and employment. Socialists would also attempt to alter the industrial structure away from the production of luxury goods toward basic consumption items and to increase basic grains output.[55]

The Reagan White House has publicly declared the Sandinistas to be communist and totalitarian and hence inimical to the United States. From the Reagan administration's perspective, the Sandinistas represent an intolerable challenge to U.S. hegemony within its traditional sphere of influence in the Western Hemisphere; the very existence of this regime is seen to undermine U.S. credibility not only in this hemisphere but around the globe.[56] The Sandinistas also stand accused by the United States of exporting revolution to neighboring Central American countries, especially, but not exclusively, El Salvador, and of entering into a military-strategic alliance with Cuba and the Soviet Union. The logical consequence of this vision has been escalating U.S. hostility toward the Sandinista regime, including sponsorship of a paramilitary war and a full-scale trade embargo.[57]

U.S. hostility has obviously created economic hardships for the Sandinistas. The contra war has been expensive in terms of human lives and destruction of crops, equipment, and infrastructure.[58] At the same time, it has provided a justification—"imperialism," "U.S. aggression"—for an increasingly authoritarian pattern of governance. The blockage of loans in the multilateral development agencies and other economic sanctions by the United States have also hurt. This bleeding of the Sandinista regime has not prevented the Sandinistas from advancing toward the consolidation of their rule. After six years of revolution, the internal opposition in Nicaragua is weak, disorganized, and demoralized. Although a serious problem, the contras are, according to most analysts, incapable of militarily defeating the Sandinista army. As matters now stand, short of a direct U.S. intervention, there is little probability that the Sandinistas will be dislodged anytime in the foreseeable future. External pressures have already propelled, and will continue to push, the regime to more authoritarian rule at home and closer links with Cuba and the Soviet Union abroad, thus undercutting hopes for democracy of any type in that country.

Conflict or Coexistence?

Can these three alternative political models coexist peacefully—in either their pure or imperfect forms—in Central America? The Reagan administration has explicitly declared that they cannot; as articulated by President Reagan himself, the goal of the U.S. government is to remove the Sandinista regime as it is currently structured. In contrast, the Contadora Group (Mexico, Venezuela, Colombia, and Panama) has affirmed that these alternative political models can live with each other.

The Reagan administration does not believe coexistence with the revolutionary model is possible for several reasons. First, President Reagan and his advisers are convinced that the Sandinista regime has become a Soviet-Cuban satellite on the American continent and constitutes a potential, if not actual, threat to U.S. strategic security. Second, they are convinced that Nicaragua has become a launching pad for aggressive subversion in Central America. Third, they believe that any agreements designed to contain Nicaragua's export of revolution would not be worth the paper they were written on unless Nicaragua first adopted a "genuine democracy": On the one hand, such agreements could not be verified; on the other, history reveals that "communists cannot be trusted to keep their word."[59] Given this interpretation of the Nicaraguan threat to U.S. vital interests, coexistence with the Sandinista regime as presently structured is impossible: For U.S. interests to be safeguarded only the removal of the current Nicaraguan government will do.

The Contadora Group recognizes that the United States does have security concerns vis-à-vis Nicaragua. It also recognizes that governments in Central America, Nicaragua included, have permitted subversive activities to be launched from their national territory against their neighbors. Contadora's proposed solution to both problems is a negotiated settlement that would provide security guarantees for all of the nations in the region as well as the United States. In contrast to the Reagan administration, they believe that adequate verification procedures can be developed (e.g., joint border patrols; periodic on-site checks by international observer teams; use of air, sea, and land-based electronic surveillance) and, thus, that coexistence with revolutionary Nicaragua would be feasible.

THE CONTADORA AFFIRMATIVE

The basic goals of Contadora can be summarized in four points: (1) the removal of foreign advisers and foreign military bases from the area; (2) a mutual and reciprocal reduction of troop levels; (3) a halt to the arms race by freezing all further arms imports; and (4) mutual nonaggression pacts among the countries in conflict. In effect, Contadora seeks to demilitarize the region and thereby remove it from the arena of East-West conflict.[60] Although the famous "twenty-one" points included in Contadora's 1983 Declaration of Principles and subsequent proposed peace treaties have embraced political pluralism and democracy, in practice Contadora has had little to say about the internal political dynamics of each country.[61]

The United States, along with all of the Central American countries, publicly backed Contadora's general objectives repeatedly over 1983 and 1984. Indeed, the Reagan administration often denounced the Sandinistas in Nicaragua during this period for refusing to accept Contadora's mediation attempts. Thus, when Nicaragua suddenly announced on September 21, 1984, that it was willing to sign the Revised Contadora Agreement without further modifications or delays, the Reagan administration was caught off-guard.[62]

Washington quickly made clear that it considered the revised agreement inadequate in several respects, particularly in the areas of verification and internal democratization, and that before any final treaty could be signed, additional modifications would have to be incorporated. Following emergency U.S. consultations with its allies in the region—Costa Rica, Honduras, and El Salvador—in late October 1984, these three countries jointly submitted to the Contadora Group a new series of modifications to be included in the agreement.[63] The proposed amendments covered four central areas: (1) tighter verification procedures to enforce the various provisions of the treaty; (2) simultaneity in the withdrawal of advisers by Cuba and the Eastern bloc countries, on the one hand, and the United States, on the other; (3) the democratization of the Sandinista regime; and (4) the right of the United States to maintain some bases and to continue joint military maneuvers with its allies in the region.[64]

Even though it appears likely that the Contadora Group will be able to incorporate amendments dealing with the issues of verification and simultaneity, predictably, those dealing with internal democratization within Nicaragua and continuation of U.S. military maneuvers and bases in the region have proven far more divisive. Even if the Contadora process does not collapse altogether, a possibility that cannot be discarded, the best that can be expected at present is a lengthy series of future negotiations without cloture.[65]

THE ALTERNATIVE OF LOW-INTENSITY WARFARE

The visible alternatives to the successful completion of a Contadora-style peace treaty are either direct intervention or low-intensity guerrilla warfare in Nicaragua. During 1985, a possible direct U.S. intervention to defeat the Sandinistas militarily surfaced as a major topic of policy debate in Washington. The U.S. military had already been authorized to conduct large-scale maneuvers in Honduras in order to prepare for such a contingency. Nevertheless, there is widespread recognition in Washington that the military and political costs of such an intervention could be high. Neither the U.S. Congress nor the bulk of U.S. public opinion currently favors such deep involvement.[66]

In the absence of a direct U.S. intervention, or an internal collapse like Grenada, the Sandinistas are likely to retain power in Nicaragua for the foreseeable future. Even with renewed U.S. assistance, most observers agree that the Honduran and Costa Rican-based contras simply will not be able to oust the Sandinistas on their own. It appears equally unlikely that the Sandinistas will be able to eliminate the 10,000 to 15,000 contras currently engaged in guerrilla warfare against their regime in the near term. The most probable scenario for Nicaragua, therefore, is prolonged, low-intensity guerrilla war against the Sandinista regime.[67]

El Salvador is in a similar situation. The incumbent government now seems able to contain the Farabundo Martí Front for National Liberation (FMLN) guerrillas. Massive increases in U.S. military assistance; new, more mobile tactics; improved leadership; and better trained and better equipped troops have permitted the government to force the guerrillas to revert for the most part from Phase II guerrilla tactics (massed attacks) to Phase I (small group action). Yet it does not appear that the Salvadoran military, even with continuing U.S. assistance, will be able to eliminate the guerrilla forces in the foreseeable future. As in Nicaragua, the most likely scenario is one of long-term, low-intensity guerrilla warfare.[68]

In both countries, then, guerrilla wars will likely drag on with profoundly negative implications for economic growth and political stability. Spillover effects have already been felt in neighboring Costa Rica and Honduras as both countries have been drawn into increasingly conflictual relations with the Sandinista government. The escalating tensions between them and Nicaragua have helped chill the business environments in all three countries, contributing to capital flight and inhibiting new private investment, domestic and foreign. As long as the current tensions persist, it is highly unlikely that these nations will be able to reactivate their economies on a sustained basis, with or without the CBI. In the absence of self-sustaining growth in Honduras and Costa Rica, extensive U.S. assistance will be required simply to keep those economies afloat. The price of continued U.S. hostility toward Nicaragua will, therefore, be retarded economic development not only in Nicaragua but in the entire region.

External Aid, Capital Swamping, and Structural Dependency

In combination, adverse economic conditions and continuing, low-intensity guerrilla warfare provide environments more propitious for regime crises and breakdowns than for the institutionalization of democracy, of whatever stripe. Moreover, they are likely to inhibit the implementation of any coherent economic strategy and thus to force an indefinite postponement of economic development. Sizable increases in U.S. economic assistance to Costa Rica, Honduras, and El Salvador have helped to keep these economies solvent and to stave off deeper economic and political difficulties in the early 1980s. This emergency aid has not, however, contributed significantly to long-term economic development.[69]

In fact, growing dependence on external assistance has raised concerns among many observers that such large amounts of financial aid cannot be absorbed productively, that Central American governments might become permanently dependent on foreign assistance simply to meet their budgetary needs, and that they may postpone reforms that could put the region on a more self-sufficient growth path. Although even the most optimistic analysts recognize that the dangers of capital swamping and structural dependency are real, at least in the short term, the optimists believe that these dangers can be managed.[70] They note that U.S. AID's requested FY 1985 annual appropriation of $1.2 billion was substantially less than the $1.5 billion that the region has lost over the last several years as a result of lower prices for coffee and sugar and higher oil import prices. Moreover, particularly because much of the aid will flow to the private sector, the immediate absorption problem is seen to be less severe. Finally, it is claimed that external assistance can be conditioned upon the recipient government committing itself to the designated economic reforms, although it is recognized that donor leverage over economic policies may be diluted if security interests are paramount.[71]

If external aid is to contribute to the consolidation of stable political regimes in the region over the longer term, however, it will be necessary for assistance flows to shift gradually from the current emphasis on emergency balance-of-payments support being used to cover current-account and fiscal deficits to more carefully targeted development projects that carry a higher long-term investment component.[72] Most importantly, if Central America is to become less dependent upon external capital inflows and resume economic development, it will have to bolster domestic savings rates. Savings rates will have to recover from the sharp declines suffered in recent years.

Less clear, however, is the preferred means for realizing that savings. Should major fiscal and administrative reforms be undertaken to transform governments into centers for savings and/or investment? Alternatively, should interest rates be raised and other financial reforms undertaken to provide greater incentives to private savers? Can private firms generate significant savings through their internal cash flow? Or, should nations seek to generate savings by accumulating a trade surplus? The answers lie partly in empirical research: For example, what is the likely response of individual savers to higher interest rates? Many of the critical choices, however, will depend upon ideological preferences. Circumstances will also dictate the range of choices available: Without a lessening of conflict in the region, greater incentives to savers are unlikely to result in the needed higher levels of domestic savings and investment.

The Sandinista government faces a dilemma similar to that of its more capitalist neighbors. Revolutionary Nicaragua has been able to survive U.S. economic pressures and stave off economic collapse through successful appeals for external assistance to Western European socialists and social democrats, the USSR and the Socialist bloc countries, Mexico, Libya, and other friendly nations.[73] Initially, the Sandinistas used external credits to maintain living standards and to avoid stabilization. More recently, they have cut back on consumption and postponed many longer-term investment projects. Nevertheless, their external and internal accounts remain out of balance and in need of foreign credits. Ironically, the contra war forces the Sandinistas to maintain and even deepen this dependence on external sources, especially those of the Socialist bloc countries.

4
Summary and Conclusions

Without peace there can be no development and without development there can be no peace: We must break this vicious cycle in the short term if we want to contribute to the maintenance of peace in Central America.[74]

—Belisario Betancur Cuartas

The roots of the current crisis in Central America do not lie in economic stagnation but rather in the structurally flawed and inequitable development models pursued during the high-growth past. Rapid but uneven economic expansion within the framework of exclusionary and illegitimate political systems generated rising levels of political disaffection and violence in Nicaragua, El Salvador, and Guatemala. The global recession of 1980-1982 and accompanying debt burdens further exacerbated tensions throughout the region. Ideological crosscurrents, spillover effects from the ongoing civil wars, and economic shocks have also increased anxieties in the region's islands of relative tranquillity—Costa Rica and Honduras. Political and economic problems have fed on each other in Central America, interacting to produce a downward spiral. If these negative trends are to be reversed, policies will be required that address both the political and economic causes of the current troubles.

After more than half a decade of economic contraction and severe political conflict, every Central American country faces the need for continuing austerity as well as painful structural adjustment to restore growth. Sharp increases in U.S. financial assistance have allowed Honduras and El Salvador to place a floor under living standards and to partially postpone economic reforms. Since U.S. AID has been willing to provide large sums on soft economic conditions, governments have been able to circumvent the IMF. In effect, governments have preferred U.S. political conditions to IMF financial stringency. Concomitantly, Nicaragua has become increasingly dependent on alternative sources of external assistance simply to maintain current levels of consumption and social services and to fend off the contras. In contrast, Guatemala and, until recently, Costa Rica have had less access to external aid and so have had to adopt more austere policies; their governments also demonstrated the political strength and will to impose stiff stabilization programs.

Overwhelmed by immediate financial and security problems, Central American governments have deferred decisions on long-term development strategies. Nevertheless, the prolonged crisis has forced many Central Americans to think more systematically about the future of their national and regional economies and what must be done to achieve more balanced, self-sustained growth.

The debate over long-term economic strategies is less polarized than the conflicts over political power. The Central American economies find themselves inserted into the global economy in similar conditions: All are small, open economies with a low technological base and a dependency on agricultural exports. Economic strategies must continue to emphasize exports based on the region's comparative advantages in good land and inexpensive labor. However, each nation does possess a somewhat different mix of national endowments, population/land ratios, and installed industrial capacity. These differences suggest that each country will also choose a somewhat different mix among the available engines for future growth: traditional agricultural exports, agroindustry, transformation industries, foodstuffs, and regionally oriented light manufacturing. Each nation will have to emphasize one or more of the export-oriented options, and nations well endowed with land may also seek self-sufficiency and even a surplus in basic grains. The dynamo of the 1960s—the Central American Common Market—will play a less central but not inconsequential role in the future provided that reforms are made in the common external tariff and in the financing of trade balances; in the meantime, intraregional trade will be facilitated by bilateral barter deals.

Summary and Conclusions

The final calculus of individual country development strategies will depend more heavily on national comparative advantage, existing productive structures, and access to markets than on ideological preferences. The political debate will focus more on instruments than ends and on the distribution of benefits among different groups in society. The sharpest divisions will occur over the relative roles that the state and the market should play in the development process, the appropriate degree of political participation in decisionmaking, and the degrees of inequality that are economically desirable and politically or morally tolerable.

Governments should avoid promising quick returns on their chosen strategies. Having indulged in foreign borrowing to postpone adjustment, Central America will have to sacrifice future consumption to meet its debt obligations. Furthermore, the near-term prospects for future capital flows and for the region's export performance leave little room for optimism. Commercial banks and foreign investors will await political peace before risking more capital (and the success of the CBI depends upon firms undertaking new investments in agroindustry and transformation industries). The IMF and the World Bank could provide more capital if governments felt strong enough to undertake major economic reforms. Even then, recovery will only be gradual.

Just as the economic crisis is forcing a rethinking of development strategies, so has political turmoil compelled a renovation of public institutions. Outside of Nicaragua, guerrilla groups and mass-based social movements may not have attained their maximum objectives, but they have served as battering rams that others are using to pry open rigid regimes. Painful upheavals have generated a fragile but hopeful trend toward political "opening" or "democratization" in the region. Every country now lays claim to democratic credentials.

After El Salvador's three elections, the consolidation of President Duarte and the Christian Democrats and the initiation of a dialogue with the FMLN-FDR (Democratic Revolutionary Front) raises the hope that democratic institutions may possibly be taking hold. Honduras is ruled by a shifting alliance between the traditional political parties and the military—although even this degree of openness is still fragile and exposed to embroilment in regional conflict. Former "pariah" Guatemala is engaged in a process of partial political liberalization. In November 1984, the Sandinistas also conducted national elections to legitimize and institutionalize their rule. Meanwhile, Costa Rica's democracy-with-justice model has weathered the first half of the 1980s without breakdown, despite strains. However limited these democratizing winds may be, that they are blowing at all represents a positive shift away from decades of personalist and military dictatorship.

The most stable regime type for the region would appear to be one or another variant of the democracy-with-justice model, undergirded by a selectively interventionist state pursuing an industrial policy. Other models face serious, although not necessarily insurmountable, obstacles. The democracy-with-liberty model suffers from fundamental legitimacy problems. The revolutionary democracy paradigm also confronts internal legitimacy problems, but it is most severely constrained, at least in the 1980s, by the hostility of a United States seeking to reassert its hegemony over the region.

Despite convergence in some respects, Central American governments currently manifest significant ideological differences. Can a *modus vivendi* be established among societies with different ideals sharing common borders? The Contadora affirmative begins with the assumption that nations with distinct internal structures can coexist providing that they recognize each other's territorial sovereignty. Even though the United States has demonstrated its power to block a Contadora accord, at least so far it has been unable to consistently implement strategies to dislodge definitively the antidemocratic right and has been unwilling to commit the power to liquidate the left: In short, the United States seems unable or unwilling to impose political homogeneity in Central America. As a result, the region seems likely to continue to experience extensive, if low-intensity, political violence and a chilly business environment. So long as such conditions persist, self-sustaining economic growth in Central America is likely to prove elusive and democratic impulses are in danger of being short-circuited. Clearly, both North Americans and Central Americans have a shared interest in peace.

Notes

1. The proceedings are summarized in "Alternative Economic Strategies for Central America and the Implications for U.S. Policy," report of a conference organized by the Overseas Development Council and The John Hopkins University School of Advanced International Studies, Washington, D.C., May 14-16, 1984.

2. On the origins and dynamics of Central America's crisis of political legitimacy, see Edelberto Torres-Rivas, "Quien Destapó la Caja de Pandora?" in Daniel Camacho and Manuel Rojas B. (eds.), *La Crisis Centroamericana*. San Jose: EDUCA and FLACSO, 1984, pp. 23-51; also Richard E. Feinberg and Robert A. Pastor, "Far from Hopeless: An Economic Program for Post-War Central America," in Robert S. Leiken (ed.), *Central America: Anatomy of Conflict*. New York: Pergamon Press, 1984, pp. 193-218.

3. United Nations Economic Commission for Latin America, *Central America: Nature of the Present Economic Crisis, the Challenges It Raises, and the International Cooperation for Which It Calls*. E/CEPAL/CCE/402/Rev.1, August 26, 1981, p. 2.

4. Solon L. Barraclough, "Agrarian Reform: Diversion or Necessity?" A paper presented at the conference on "Alternative Economic Strategies for Central America and the Implications for U.S. Policy," Washington, D.C., May 14-26, 1984, p. 21.

5. See Table 3. Also Rodrigo Moscoso, "The Central American Region." A paper presented at the conference on "Alternative Economic Strategies for Central America and the Implications for U.S. Policy," Washington, D.C., May 14-26, 1984, pp. 2-3.

6. See Richard E. Feinberg, Richard Newfarmer, and Bernadette Orr, "Caribbean Basin Initiative: Pros and Cons," in Mark Falcoff and Robert Royal (eds.), *Crisis and Opportunity: U.S. Policy in Central America and the Caribbean*. Washington, D.C.: Ethics and Public Policy Center, 1984, pp. 101-118.

7. Luis Rene Caceres, "Toward a Strategy for the Economic Reactivation of Central America." A paper presented at the conference on "Alternative Economic Strategies for Central America and the Implications for U.S. Policy," Washington, D.C., May 14-16, 1984.

8. See Henry Kissinger, et al., *The Report of the National Bipartisan Commission on Central America*. Washington, D.C.: U.S. Government Printing Office, 1984.

9. Personal interviews, San Jose, Costa Rica, January 1985.

10. On aid to Nicaragua, see Michael E. Conroy, "External Dependence, External Assistance, and Economic Aggression Against Nicaragua." Notre Dame: Kellogg Institute, Working Paper no. 27, July 1984; the $400-500 million figure is based on estimates obtained by the authors in Managua in January 1985.

11. See George Grayson, "The San Jose Oil Facility," *Third World Quarterly* (vol. 7, no. 2) April 1985. By late 1984 the Soviet Union had replaced Mexico as Nicaragua's leading oil supplier while Venezuela had halted all deliveries to the Sandinista regime.

12. Moscoso, "The Central American Region."

13. World Bank, *Annual Reports*, Washington, D.C.: World Bank, various years.

14. Central American Bank for Economic Integration, "Financial Outlook of the Central American Bank for Economic Integration," mimeo, November 1984, p. 4.

15. Personal interviews, Managua, Nicaragua, January 1985.

16. Cámaras de Comercio e Industria de Guatemala, *Análisis de la Situación Económica de Guatemala, 1965-1984*. Guatemala City: Cámaras, 1984, Table 6, pp. 96-97.

17. Personal interviews, San Salvador, El Salvador, and Managua, Nicaragua, January 1985.

18. Consejeros Económicos y Financieros (CEFSA), "Costa Rica: Indicadores Económicos, 1978-84," mimeo, November 14, 1984, p. 2.

19. See Joan Nelson, "The Politics of Stabilization," in Richard E. Feinberg and Valeriana Kallab (eds.), *Adjustment Crisis in the Third World*. New Brunswick: Transaction Books and Overseas Development Council, 1984, pp. 99-118.

20. For a description of the Costa Rican stabilization program, see Richard E. Feinberg, "Costa Rica: The End of the Fiesta," in Richard E. Newfarmer (ed.), *From Gunboats to Diplomacy*. Baltimore: The Johns Hopkins University Press, 1984.

21. Comisión Económica para América Latina y el Caribe (CEPAL), *Balance Preliminar de la Economía Latinoamericana Durante 1984*. Santiago: CEPAL, 1984, Tables 10 and 11.

22. Increased government intervention in trade and financial markets is a common response to economic crises. See Richard E. Feinberg, "LDC Debt and the Public Sector," *Challenge*, July/August 1985, pp. 27-34.

23. Personal interviews in Central America, January 1985.

24. The U.S. General Accounting Office (GAO) revealed that the U.S. Treasury Department and the Office of Management and Budget have preferred more emphasis on economic reforms but have often been overruled by the State Department. *Providing Effective Economic Assistance to El Salvador and Honduras: A Formidable Task*. Washington, D.C.: GAO, NSIAD-85-82, July 3, 1985, 73 p.

25. An interesting discussion of these issues can be found in Bill Gibson, "The Limits of Terms-of-Trade Policy in Post-Revolutionary Nicaragua," University of Massachusetts at Amherst, mimeo, August 1984.

26. A balanced study of effective levels of protection and the need for tariff rationalization is found in Prodesarrollo, *Estructura de la Protección al Sector Industrial en Costa Rica*. San Jose: Disegraf Fernando Arce, 1984, p. 212

27. Costa Rican Ministry of National Planning, *Plan Nacional de Desarrollo, 1982-86: "Volvamos a la Tierra,"* vol. 1. San Jose, Costa Rica: MIDEPLAN, 1983, pp. 7-48.

28. Jaime Wheelock Roman, *Entre la Crisis y la Agresión*. Managua: Comunicaciones MINDRA, 1984, p. 147.

29. USAID, *Guatemala: Country Development Strategy Statement, FY 1986*. Washington, D.C.: USAID, 1984, Table 18, p. 41.

30. Nicaraguan Ministry of Planning, mimeo, 1984.

31. Costa Rican Ministry of National Planning, *Plan Nacional*, vol. 1, p. 71.

32. Wheelock Roman, *Entre la Crisis y la Agresión,*, p. 37.

33. USAID, *Guatemala*, Table 18, p. 41.

34. Furthermore, on November 2, 1984, the five Central American representatives or governors to the Inter-American Development Bank met in San Jose, Costa Rica, and collectively agreed to petition IDB President Antonio Ortiz Mena to organize a consultative group for Central America that would include the major external donors active in the region.

35. See Banco Centroamericano de Integración Económica, "El Presente y Futuro del BCIE." A paper presented at the conference on "Centroamerica y la Capitalizacion del BCIE," Cartagena, Colombia, November 28-30, 1984, p. 27.

36. USAID, *Honduras Country Development Strategy Statement*, FY 1986. Washington, D.C.: USAID, 1984, p. 33.

37. Inter-American Development Bank, "Informe Económico: Nicaragua." Washington, D.C.: IDB, mimeo, October 1984, Table 11, p. 20.

38. Perhaps because of its limited political/electoral appeal, Central American politicans and intelligentsia have not to our knowledge written any fully elaborated justifications of this conservative view of the state.

39. On the advocacy of supply-side economics in some Central and Latin American circles, see Jon Basil Utley, "Supply-side Conference in Latin America," *Washington Inquirer*, March 15, 1985, p. 11.

40. See, for example, Claudio Gonzalez-Vega, "Central America: Foreign Assistance, Policy Reforms, and Domestic Financial Markets in Reconstruction and Growth." A paper presented at the conference on "Alternative Economic Strategies for Central America and the Implications for U.S. Policy," Washington, D.C., May 14–16, 1984.

41. This argument is developed by Claudio Gonzalez-Vega, *Temor al Ajuste: Los Costos Sociales de las Políticas Económicas en Costa Rica Durante la Década de los 70*. San Jose: Academia de Centroamrica, Study Series 2, 1984, p. 48.

42. Personal interviews, San Salvador, El Salvador, January 1985. Roberto D'Aubuisson and his ultra-right wing ARENA party are increasingly seen as a liability by former conservative supporters. Because of U.S. pressures and President Duarte's strong showing in the March 31, 1985, elections, many Salvadoran conservative groups appear inclined to work with Duarte to moderate any leftward movement rather than oppose him outright.

43. For background on the role of the right and the military in Guatemala see Central American and Caribbean Program, *Report on Guatemala: Findings of the Study Group on United States-Guatemalan Relations*. SAIS Papers in International Affairs, no. 7. Boulder: Westview Press, 1985. On the "democratic opening" in that country see Loren Jenkins, "Guatemala Gears Up for Uncertain Vote," *The Washington Post*, December 26, 1984, p. A31; James LeMonye, "Guatemala Fights Its Bad-boy Image," *The New York Times*, December 25, 1984. And Richard Millett, "Guatemala: Progress and Paralysis," *Current History*, March 1985, pp. 109–113, 136.

44. Costa Rica represents the archetype of the democracy-with-justice model. On the Costan Rican system, see Charles F. Denton, *Patterns of Costa Rican Politics*. Boston: Allyn and Bacon, 1971; Mitchell A. Seligson, *Peasants of Costa Rica and the Development of Agrarian*

Capitalism. Madison: University of Wisconsin Press, 1980; Charles D. Ameringer, *Democracy in Costa Rica*. New York: Praeger, 1982; José Luis Vega C., *Poder Político y Democracia en Costa Rica*. San Jose: Editorial Porvenir S.A., 1982, pp. 113-136; and Chester Zelaya, et al., *Democracia en Costa Rica? Cinco Opiniones Polémicas*. San Jose: Editorial Universidad Estatal a Distancia, 1983.

45. See, for example, Fernando Berrocal, "La Crisis Económica Internacional y la Integración Centroamericana," in José Miguel Alfaro, et al., *Centroamérica: Condiciones para su Integración*. San Jose: Ediciones FLACSO, 1982, pp. 137-150; José Miguel Alfaro, "La Integración como Instrumento de Desarrollo," in ibid., pp. 111-122; and Eduardo Lizano and Minor Sagot, *Costa Rica y la Integración Económica Centroamericana*. San Jose: Academia de Centroamérica, Study Center 1, 1984.

46. The general rationale for activist state intervention in LDCs is elaborated on by Richard Feinberg, *The Intemperate Zone: The Third World Challenge to U.S. Foreign Policy*. New York: W.W. Norton, 1983, pp. 101-109. For the Costa Rican case see Lizano and Sagot, *Costa Rica*, pp. 77-94. Also Luis Rene Caceres, "Toward a Strategy for the Economic Reactivation of Central America." A paper presented at the conference on "Alternative Economic Strategies for Central America and the Implications for U.S. Policy," Washington, D.C., May 14-16, 1984.

47. Personal interviews in Costa Rica, Guatemala, and El Salvador, January 1985.

48. Eduardo Lizano, "Regional Integration: Can the Central American Common Market Be Revived?" A paper presented at the conference on "Alternative Economic Strategies for Central America and the Implications for U.S. Policy," Washington, D.C., May 14-16, 1984, pp. 1-2.

49. For an analysis of the "crisis" in Costa Rica, see Manuel Rojas B., "Costa Rica: El Fin de una Era," in Daniel Camacho and Manuel Rojas B. (eds.), *La Crisis Centroamericana*. San Jose: FLACSO-EDUCA, 1984, pp. 126-151.

50. On recent trends in Honduras, see Phillip Shepard, "The USS Honduras," *St. Louis Post Dispatch*, January 13, 1985; John B. Oakes, "Treating Honduras as a Vassal State," *The New York Times*, January 11, 1985; and Thomas P. Anderson, "Honduras in Transition," *Current History*, March 1985, pp. 114-117, 132.

51. For sympathetic discussions of the Sandinista political project, see José Luis Coraggio, "Revolución y Democracia en Nicaragua." Managua: INIES/CRIES, Cuadernos de Pensamiento Propio, 1984, pp.

9–31; Humberto Ortega Saavedra, *Sobre la Insurrección*. Mexico: Editorial Nuestro Tiempo, 1980; and Xabier Gorostiaga, "Los Dilemas de la Revolución Popular Sandinista." Managua: INIES/CRIES, Cuadernos de Pensamiento Propio, 1982.

52. See José Lobo, "Nicaragua's Economic Crisis," *CUSLAR Newsletter*, March-April, 1985, pp. 1–8; Victor Tirado, "Nuestro Concepto de la Economía Mixta," *Barricada*, February 16, 1985; Alfonso Dubois, "La Economia Mixta en la Transicion en Nicaragua: El Caso del Azúcar." Managua: INIES, 1983; Comandante Jaime Wheelock, "Es Urgente Estabilizar y Ordenar Nuestra Economía," *Barricada*, February 14, 1985.

53. Corragio, "Revolución y Democracia," pp. 30–32; also Richard Fagen, "Revolution and Crisis in Nicaragua," in Martin Diskin (ed.), *Trouble in Our Backyard: Central America and the United States in the Eighties*. New York: Pantheon Books, 1983, pp. 125–154.

54. Wheelock Roman, *Entre la Crisis y la Agresión*, pp. 59–98.

55. Personal interviews, Central America, January 1985.

56. Jeane S. Kirkpatrick, "This Time We Know What's Happening," in Mark Falcoff and Robert Royal (eds.), *Crisis and Opportunity*, pp. 165–172.

57. The list of Reagan administration denunciations of the Sandinista regime is found in U.S. Department of State, *Broken Promises: Sandinista Repression of Human Rights in Nicaragua*. Washington: U.S. State Department report, October 1984. President Reagan has set out his administration's views on the question of U.S. interests in Central America on numerous occasions. See, for example, his April 27, 1983, speech to a Joint Session of Congress entitled "Central America: Defending Our Vital Interests," in U.S. Department of State (ed.), *Realism, Strength, Negotiation: Key Foreign Policy Statements of the Reagan Administration*. Washington: Bureau of Public Affairs, U.S. State Department, May 1984, pp. 128–131; or his televised address to the nation on May 9, 1984, entitled "U.S. Interests in Central America," in the same volume.

The CIA-backed "covert war" against the Sandinista regime was authorized by President Reagan in November 1981 with initial funding of $18 million. By late 1984 when funding for the contras was halted by the Democrat-controlled U.S. House of Representatives, approximately $80 million had been approved by Congress. In addition, the contras have been able to operate from bases in Honduras with the tacit approval of the Honduran military and have been given access to U.S. military equipment left behind after U.S. military maneuvers held in Honduras. When administration requests for "humanitarian" aid were temporarily turned down by the House in April 1985, Washington proceeded to impose a trade embargo on Nicaragua by executive order in May.

58. In September 1985 in the World Court, the Sandinistas requested a $375 million judgment against the United States as "minimum" reparations for the contra war.

59. The quote is from CIA Director William Casey. See Philip Beglin, "Casey and 'Focus of Evil'," *The Washington Post*, June 17, 1985, p. 11.

60. On the objectives of Contadora see Bruce Michael Bagley, Roberto Alvarez, and Katherine Hagedorn (eds.), *Contadora and the Central American Peace Process: Selected Documents*. Boulder: Westview Press, 1985.

61. The question of internal democracy is a knotty one for the Contadora group for at least two reasons. First, in principle, its members all endorse the right of self-determination and respect for the sovereignty of every nation. Behind these principles, of course, lie historic fears of U.S. intervention in the region. Second, not all the Contadora countries are in fact "democratic." Mexico, in particular, is a one-party dominant state—an inclusionary authoritarian regime—and would not object to the conversion of the Sandinistas into a type of left-wing PRI and the regime into a one-party dominant, authoritarian system similar to Mexico's. Venezuela, in contrast, places much more emphasis on pluralist democracy. Contadora purposely left this issue vague to avoid internal dissension.

62. Some observers have questioned the sincerity of Nicaragua's commitment to Contadora, arguing that the Sandinistas announced their willingness to sign the Revised Act without modifications only to win favorable publicity: They knew full well that the United States and its allies in the region would never agree to a treaty that did not include adequate provisions for verification and democratization. Less conspiratorial analyses point out that the Sandinistas recognized the act as the best deal they could get: Peace with their neighbors and the United States in exchange for halting all export of revolution, thus guaranteeing the survival of the Sandinista regime.

63. The Sandinistas sometimes dismiss these countries as little more than "stalking horses" or "satellites" of the United States because of their dependence on U.S. economic and military assistance. This position clearly glosses over the real security concerns of the governing elites of Nicaragua's neighbors. The United States did press its allies on the Revised Act, but it did not have to convince them of the wisdom of more effective verification procedures and other amendments

to the Contadora document. Honduras, for example, is especially keen on the maintenance of U.S. military bases and the continuance of joint maneuvers. El Salvador seeks ironclad guarantees that Nicaragua will cease all support for the FMLN guerrillas. Many Costa Ricans fear Sandinista military incursions, the export of guerrilla violence, and more subtle forms of Marxist politico-ideological influence.

64. See Juan M. Vasquez, "Contadora Officials to Try to Revive Latin Peace Effort," *Los Angeles Times*, January 7, 1985; "Revised Latin Pact Ready for Regional Talks," *Los Angeles Times*, January 10, 1985.

65. This pessimistic interpretation is widely shared by both government officials and independent analysts in Mexico City, Bogota, and Caracas. The Contadora process will continue, primarily because none of the parties want to bear the onus of having been the first to withdraw. However, unless and until the United States and Nicaragua reach some accommodation, an increasingly dim prospect, Contadora will not advance.

66. A June 2, 1985, *The New York Times*/CBS News poll showed that 53 percent of the U.S. public opposed U.S. aid for the contras while only 32 percent supported it. Even higher percentages opposed the direct use of U.S. troops in Central America. Adam Clymer, "Most Americans in Survey Oppose Aid for Overthrow of Sandinistas," *The New York Times*, June 5, 1985, p. 48. Although recognizing that U.S. public opinion does not favor deepening U.S. military involvement in Central America, on May 23, 1985, Secretary of State George Shultz warned members of Congress that if they did not approve renewed aid for the American-backed Nicaraguan rebels, "they are hastening the day where the threat will grow, and we will be faced with an agonizing choice about the use of U.S. combat troops." Following Secretary Shultz's comments, top administration officials were quoted in *The New York Times* to the effect that the United States did have "contingency" plans for invading Nicaragua and that a U.S. strike could be quickly successful. U.S. military leaders had previously rejected the notion that Nicaragua could be invaded easily or quickly. See Bill Keller, "U.S. Military Is Termed Prepared for Any Move Against Nicaragua," *The New York Times*, June 4, 1985, p. A1. See also Joanne Omang, "Hill Tensions Rise on Nicaragua," *The Washington Post*, June 10, 1985.

67. General Paul Gorman, former head of the U.S. Southern Command based in Panama and a key military advisor to the Reagan administration for Central America, stated in his final testimony to Congress before resigning that, despite progress, no quick victory by the contras could be expected in Nicaragua and the guerrilla war in

that country might continue for years. See Bill Keller, "U.S. General Says Nicaragua Rebels Cannot Win Soon," *The New York Times*, February 28, 1985, p. A1. There have been a number of news reports alleging that El Salvador, Honduras, and Israel, all major recipients of U.S. foreign assistance, have provided aid to the contras. A variety of conservative organizations in the United States—e.g., Civilian Military Assistance (CMA), *The Washington Times*, and the Young Republicans—have done fundraising or provided equipment, food, and medical supplies. Various wealthy Nicaraguan exiles in Miami and other sympathetic "philanthropists" from the United States, Latin America, Europe, and the Middle East have contributed to the contras' cause. See, for example, Alfonso Chardy, "Contras Get Increasing Private Aid," *The Miami Herald*, January 21, 1985; David Ignatius and David Rogers, "Aiding the Contras," *The Wall Street Journal*, March 6, 1985.

68. Conservative columnists Rowland Evans and Robert Novak have raised the spectre of "the horrors of another 20 years of war" in El Salvador unless "effective pressure is brought to bear on Nicaragua." See "El Salvador: 20 More Years of War?" *The Washington Post*, May 29, 1985, p. A21. Although President Duarte and his Christian Democratic Party began a process of "dialogue" with the FDR-FMLN leaders in La Palma and Ayagualo in 1984, interviews in San Salvador in January 1985 indicated that most analysts doubted that the talks would produce a negotiated settlement in the foreseeable future.

69. Jim Leach, George Miller, and Mark Hatfield, "U.S. Aid to El Salvador, A report to the Arms Control and Foreign Policy Caucus." Washington, D.C.: mimeo, February 1985, p. 66.

70. James W. Fox, "Financial Needs for Central American Development." A paper presented at the conference on "Alternative Economic Strategies for Central America and the Implications for U.S. Policy," Washington, D.C., May 14-16, 1984, pp. 4-7.

71. Ibid., pp. 7-10; also Viron Vaky, "Reagan's Central American Policy: An Isthmus Restored," in Leiken, *Central America*, pp. 237-242.

72. This was a consensus conclusion among the participants in the "Alternative Economic Strate gies" conference sponsored by ODC and SAIS in May 1984. See the rapporteurs' report cited in note 1.

73. Despite a clear Soviet presence in Nicaragua, most evidence indicates that the USSR is moving cautiously in terms of both military and economic aid. Since 1979, military assistance to the Sandinistas from the Soviet bloc has totaled about $500 million. It began as a $5 million grant in 1979, rose to $7 million in 1980, and increased to

$45 million in 1981, as the Reagan administration launched the "covert war" in November 1981. Economic aid appears to have peaked in 1982 at $253 million and then dropped back to $146 million in 1983 and 1984. The Soviet bloc is playing an increasing role in Nicaragua trade, but until its 1985 embargo, the United States was still Nicaragua's single largest trading partner, accounting for about 20 percent of Nicaragua's imports and a similar percentage of its exports.

In the wake of U.S. economic sanctions against Nicaragua in April 1985 and the subsequent renewal of U.S. "humanitarian" aid to the contras, it seems likely that the Soviet Union and the Eastern European countries will step up their assistance to Nicaragua. Nevertheless, most analysts agree that, given Angola, Afghanistan, Poland, and Soviet economic problems at home, there are real limits to what the Soviets will do for the Sandinistas economically or militarily. Clifford Krauss and Robert S. Greenberger, "Despite Fears of U.S., Soviet Aid to Nicaragua Appears to Be Limited," *The Wall Street Journal*, April 3, 1985, p. 1; and Stephen Kinzer, "Sandinistas Are Showing Surprising Staying Power." *The New York Times*, June 9, 1985, p. E3.

74. From an address entitled "Centroamérica en Medio del Torbellino," delivered by the Colombian president on November 28, 1984, in Cartagena, Colombia.

List of Conference Participants

"Alternative Economic Strategies for Central America and the Implications for U.S. Policy"
Washington, D.C.
May 14–16, 1984

José Miguel Alfaro, a former vice president of Costa Rica, is a practicing attorney, professor of political science on the Law Faculty at the University of Costa Rica, and a trustee of the University for Peace.

Sven Arndt is the resident scholar and director of the International Trade Project of the American Enterprise Institute.

Bruce M. Bagley is associate professor of comparative politics and acting director of the Latin American Studies Program of The Johns Hopkins University School of Advanced International Studies.

Solon Barraclough is director of the United Nations Research Institute for Social Development, Geneva, Switzerland.

Luis Rene Caceres works at the Central American Bank for Economic Integration in Tegucigalpa, Honduras.

William Cline is senior fellow at the Institute for International Economics, Washington, D.C.

Conference Participants

Jorge del Canto is international consultant at the Bank of America, Washington, D.C.

Richard E. Feinberg is vice president of the Overseas Development Council, Washington, D.C.

James W. Fox works in the Office of Development and Programming in the Bureau of Latin America and the Caribbean at the U.S. Agency for International Development.

Claudio Gonzales-Vega is visiting professor of economics at Ohio State University and professor of economics at the University of Costa Rica.

Louis W. Goodman is senior program associate of the Latin American Program of the Woodrow Wilson International Center for Scholars, Washington, D.C.

Xabier Gorostiaga is director of the Institute of Economic and Social Research (INIES) in Managua, Nicaragua.

Richard Hough is a rural development consultant for the American Institute for Free Labor Development (AIFLD).

Eduardo Lizano is president of the Central Bank of Costa Rica.

Constantine Menges is special assistant to the president and senior director of Latin American Affairs at the National Security Council.

Rodrigo Moscoso is deputy manager of the operations department at the Inter-American Development Bank.

Roberto Murray-Meza is president of La Constancia, S.A., and president of the Salvadoran Foundation for Economic and Social Development (FUSADES), San Salvador, El Salvador.

Clark Reynolds is director of the Project on United States–Mexico Relations at the Food Research Institute at Stanford University and founder of the Monticello West Foundation.

Manuel Sevilla is professor of economics at the Catholic University of San Salvador, El Salvador.

Alan Stoga, a consultant to the Kissinger Commission on economic issues, is senior associate at Kissinger Associates.

Joseph T. Thome is professor of law at the University of Wisconsin-Madison and research associate of the Land Tenure Center of the same university.

José Luis Vega-Carballo is head of the unit of Technical Assistance in the Ministry of the Presidency in Costa Rica and professor of political sociology at the University of Costa Rica.

Francisco Villagran Kramer, former vice president of Guatemala, is a consultant to the Inter-American Development Bank.

Other Books Published by
the Overseas Development Council

Development Strategies Reconsidered, John P. Lewis and contributors (1986)

Investing in Development: New Roles for Private Capital? Theodore H. Moran and contributors (1986)

Between Two Worlds: The World Bank in the Coming Decade, Richard E. Feinberg and contributors (1986)

The United States and Mexico: Face to Face with New Technology, Cathryn L. Thorup and contributors (1986)

U.S. Foreign Policy and the Third World: Agenda 1985-86, edited by John W. Sewell, Richard E. Feinberg, and Valeriana Kallab (1985)

Hard Bargaining Ahead: U.S. Trade Policy and Developing Countries, edited by Ernest H. Preeg (1985)

Africa's Struggle for Sustained Development, Helen C. Low (1985)

*Other Books Published by
the Latin American Studies Program,
School of Advanced International Studies
The Johns Hopkins University*

Fleeing the Maelstrom: Central American Refugees, Patricia Weiss Fagen and Sergio Aguayo (available through SAIS CACP; 1986)

Selected Essays on Cuba, Wayne S. Smith (available through SAIS CACP; 1986)

The Private Sector in Cuban Agriculture, 1959-1985: A Socio-Economic Study, Lauren A. Burnhill (available through SAIS CACP; 1985)

Colombian Foreign Policy in the 1980s: The Search for Leverage, Bruce Michael Bagley and Juan Gabriel Tokatlian (available through SAIS CACP; 1985)

Contadora and the Central American Peace Process, edited by Bruce Michael Bagley, Roberto Alvarez, and Katherine J. Hagedorn (available through Westview Press; 1985)

The Sistema Aliemtario Mexicano: An Economic and Political Analysis of Mexican Food Policy, 1980-1982, Paul Haber and Mark Nechodom (available through SAIS CACP; 1985)

Report on Guatemala: Findings of the Study Group on United States-Guatemalan Relations, edited by the Central American and Caribbean Program, SAIS (available through Westview Press; 1985)

The Transformation of the Educational System in Cuba, José R. Fernandez (available through SAIS CACP; 1985)